D0506525

Embroidery
to Embellish Everything

Embroidery
to Embellish Everything

30 NEW HAND-STITCHED DESIGNS

SHARON AND KRISTIN JANKOWICZ

**Creative Publishing
international**

Chanhassen, MN

**Creative Publishing
international**

Copyright 2006
Creative Publishing international
18705 Lake Drive East
Chanhassen, Minnesota 55317
1-800-328-3895
www.creativepub.com
All rights reserved

President/CEO: Ken Fund
Vice President/Retail Sales: Kevin Haas

Executive Editor: Alison Brown Cerier
Senior Editor: Linda Neubauer
Photo Stylist: Joanne Wawra
Creative Director: Brad Springer
Photo Art Director: Tim Himsel
Photographer: Steve Galvin
Production Manager: Linda Halls

Cover Design: Brian Donahue / bedesign, inc.
Page Design and Layout: Brian Donahue / bedesign, inc.

Library of Congress Cataloging-in-Publication Data

Jankowicz, Sharon.
  Embroidery to embellish everything / Sharon
and Kristin Jankowicz.
    p. cm.
ISBN 1-58923-254-2 (soft cover)
  1. Embroidery. I. Jankowicz, Kristin. II. Title.
  TT770.J35 2006
  746.44—dc22
              2005028232

Printed in China

10 9 8 7 6 5 4 3 2 1

Sharon and Kristin Jankowicz, mother and daughter, design projects for the craft industry. Each a professional graphic designer and versatile needle-crafter, they are a witty, dynamic design duo. Every project created in their Illinois studio has the fingerprints of both all over it.

Contents

THIS BOOK IS FOR YOU IF   6

HOW TO USE THIS BOOK   7

The Designs   8

Sun Star   8
Heart Flash   10
Fish Fossil   12
The Big Kahuna   14
Dirty Martini   16
Royal Beast   18
Spiral (Embroidered)   20
Spiral (Appliqué)   22
Sizzling Serpent   24
Bo Ho Beaded Border   26
Baroque Cross   28
Ankh Amulet   30
Dress Like an Egyptian   32
Butterflies   34
Time Flies   36
Crown Jewels   38
Steamy   40
Crabby   42
Happy Herbivore   44
Team Spirit "10"   46
Almost Argyle   48
Love   50
Sweet Confection   52
Wedding Keepsake   54
Eiffel Tower   56
Note Book   58
Celebration   60
Party Balloon   62
Scrapbook Frames   64
Scrapbook Pocket   66

It's Easy When You Know How   68

GET READY   68
Fabrics • Threads • Needles • Cutting
Tools • Notions • Tools and Tips for
Pattern Transfer • Hoops

GET SET   77
Prepare the Floss or Thread • Thread the
Needle • Tips for Good Stitches • Knots
and Tails • Finishing Touch

STITCH   82
Straight Stitches • Running Stitches • Satin
Stitch • Couching • Coral Stitch • Chain
Stitches • Blanket Stitches • French Knots
• Backstitches • Split Stitch • Stem Stitches

GET CREATIVE   94
Add Beads • Add Paint • Stitch on Paper
and Cardstock

The Patterns   97

SOURCES   112

This Book Is for You If

. . .

YOU love the trendy thread-embellished looks, especially the one-of-a-kind accessories in boutiques. You, yes you, can make your own embellishments that are even better.

You have been searching for fresh new and fun designs to stitch.

YOU want to make a special gift for a family member or friend. Nothing says "I love you" like a hand-stitched present.

You love to add your personal touch. These designs are made to be customized. Put them wherever you want them. Change the colors, change the stitches, add some beads or paint, combine designs.

YOU don't want to make a major investment in a new craft. The supplies for embroidery are simple and inexpensive.

You have been known to start craft projects but not finish them (despite best intentions). We understand. We engineered these designs to be "finishable" in a short time.

YOU are a newbie, but you don't want your projects to show it. All the stitches we use can be mastered even by beginners, and the tips, photos, and drawings we offer will help you get results that will make you look like a pro.

You are a scrapbooker, card maker, or paper artist. You can stitch any of these designs on paper or cardstock—and we'll tell you how.

YOU are always on the go. These projects are portable; pop one in a bag and take it everywhere you go.

You need some serious relaxation. There won't be complicated stitch charts to follow. So you can stitch while listening to music, visiting with a friend, even watching a movie. Sit back, take your time, relax, and unwind.

. . .

How to Use this Book

...

There are thirty original needlework designs that are fresh, fun, and fast to finish. You'll have step-by-step instructions and a close-up photograph of each design. Also, we stitched each design on something to wear, something for the home, or a paper craft like a gift card or scrapbook page, so you can see the designs "in action." You'll see lots of ideas for where to place the designs.

We stitched up the designs in fabulous threads, including the new metallics and linen lines. Some designs are enhanced with beads or fabric paints. In the materials list for each project, you will find the type of thread and general colors we used. Specific brand names and color numbers are listed in Sources, page 112. You can use our choices or follow your imagination and take the designs in your own direction. Enlarged photos of each design help you see the details, but remember that your stitches will be smaller, in proportion to the original size of the patterns which begin on page 98.

Any of the designs can be embroidered on fabric, craft foam, or paper. Enlarge or reduce the designs on a computer or copy machine to any size you want. Embroider single designs or use multiples. Feel free to reverse designs that are asymmetrical. Embroider the designs in different stitches to give them different texture. Pick threads in your own color combinations and add embellishments you choose.

There are step-by-step instructions for stitching each design. You'll find the patterns at the back of the book. But before you start stitching, we really recommend that you read through the section It's Easy When You Know How, which begins on page 68. That's the how-to section that will tell you everything you need to know,

from choosing threads and tools to basic stitching. There are tips to help you stitch on fabrics and on papers, as well as directions for the stitches used in the book, with how-to drawings and photos. Before you know it, you'll be stitching away and loving it.

...

Sharon and Kristin

Sun Star

This hot sun star has universal appeal. It is a radiant embellishment that will brighten almost anything. The sample was stitched on a sensual silk blouse, which is a great fabric choice for beginners. Because silk is smooth and stable, the needle glides through, making it easy to perfect your stitches.

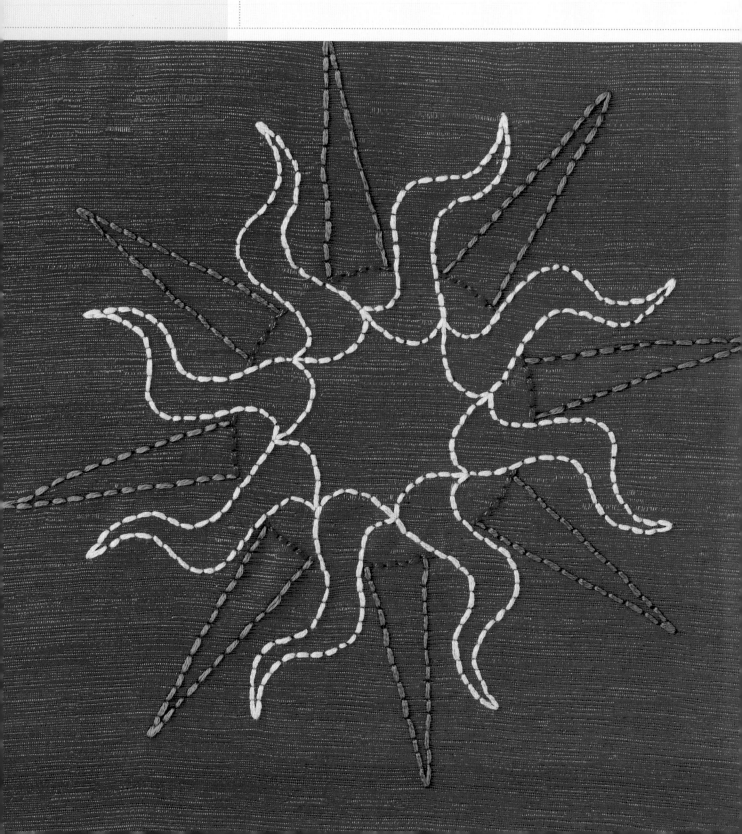

1. Copy the pattern (page 97), and transfer it onto the fabric.

2. Put the fabric in a hoop.

3. *Backstitch* the very inside of the sun, using yellow pearl thread.

4. *Backstitch* the curvy rays of the sun, using yellow pearl thread.

5. *Backstitch* the long straight rays of the sun, using bright blue pearl thread.

6. *Backstitch* the base of each blue ray, using plum pearl thread.

You'll need

✓ Something to embroider

✓ Tools/materials for transferring the design

✓ Embroidery hoop, 8" (20.5 cm) diameter

✓ Cotton pearl thread, size 5: yellow, bright blue, and plum

✓ Chenille needle, size 22

✓ Embroidery scissors

Stitch Tip

To protect very delicate fabrics like silk or satin, place tissue over the fabric before securing the hoop. Tear away the center of the tissue to expose the area that you'll embroider.

Heart Flash

Create a tattoo design with a different kind of needle and a lot less pain! Stitch this heart on a black T-shirt like this one, and add some paint if you're in the mood. You can add some words, too. How about this design on a baby boy's tank top with "My Girl" stitched on the banner and a great big "MOM" in the heart?

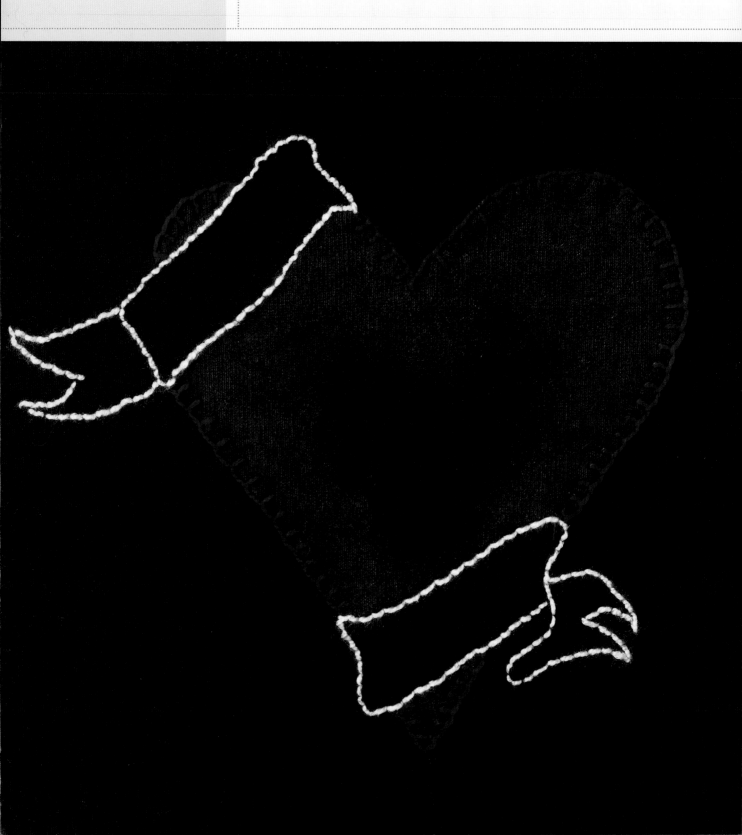

1. Copy the pattern (page 98), and transfer it onto the fabric.

2. Transfer the pattern onto a piece of cardstock and cut out only the heart areas (be sure not to cut the ribbon), so you have a stencil to use for painting.

3. Mix the red paint with the textile medium to create fabric paint, following the directions on the bottle of textile medium.

4. Place the stencil over the transferred design on the fabric, and secure the edges with tape. Place a piece of scrap paper under the fabric to keep the paint from bleeding through.

5. Dip the tip of the stencil brush into the red fabric paint and blot the excess paint off on a piece of scrap paper. Dab red paint onto the fabric, beginning at the outer edges of the stencil and gradually moving inward as the brush runs out of paint. Repeat until you have shaded the entire perimeter of the heart.

6. Remove the stencil and let the paint dry for several hours.

7. Put the fabric in a hoop. *Blanket stitch* around the edges of the heart, using red pearl thread.

8. *Backstitch* the ribbons, using white pearl thread.

You'll need

- Something to embroider
- Tools/materials for transferring the design
- Scraps of cardstock
- Craft scissors or shears
- Craft knife
- Self-healing cutting mat
- Acrylic craft paint: red
- Textile medium
- Tape
- Fabric stencil brush, size ½" (1.3 cm)
- Embroidery hoop, 8" (20.5 cm) diameter
- Cotton pearl thread, size 5: red and white
- Chenille needle, size 22
- Embroidery scissors

Stitch Tip

Omit steps 2 to 6 if you don't want to paint the heart.

Fish Fossil

This is a dynamite design for beginners. It uses only one easy stitch, and the whole design can be completed in about an hour. You'll be finished so fast, you might want to sew a whole school of fish fossils in different sizes. We embroidered the fish onto a pair of surf shorts. A larger fish would look great chain stitched onto a beach towel.

1. Copy the pattern (page 98), and transfer it onto the fabric.

2. Put the fabric in a hoop.

3. *Backstitch* the fish fossil, using yellow-green pearl thread.

4. *Backstitch* the outline, using ivory pearl thread.

(page 98)

You'll need

✓ Something to embroider

✓ Tools/materials for transferring the design

✓ Embroidery hoop

✓ Cotton pearl thread, size 5: yellow-green and ivory

✓ Chenille needle, size 22

✓ Embroidery scissors

Stitch Tip

An outline "echo" like the one around this fish fossil highlights the design and adds a little textural interest to your embroidery. Choose a color for the echo that matches the background fabric.

The Big Kahuna

Get tropical with this exotic tiki man. With this good luck totem embroidered on your board trunks, you're ready to catch the big wave. And dude, the big kahuna would look awesome on a beach bag, towel, or tropical themed home and party décor.

1. Copy the pattern (page 99), and transfer it onto the fabric.

2. Put the fabric in a hoop.

3. Thread the chenille needle with gold-olive pearl thread. Working from top to bottom, *backstitch* two rows close together at the very top of the hat, one row on the cheeks, top of the nostrils, two middle rings of the mouth, lower jaws, and center tier of the base. *Stem stitch* in a circle around the second tier (counting from the bottom) of the base.

4. Thread the chenille needle with red-orange pearl thread. *Satin stitch* the triangle and hatband. *Backstitch* the earring with very small stitches.

5. Thread the chenille needle with beige-gray pearl thread. *Backstitch* the two sides of the hat and the top tier of the base. *Stem stitch* the ears and fourth tier of the base. *Straight stitch* the lines on the cheeks with six long stitches on each side.

6. Thread the chenille needle with lemon yellow pearl thread. *Backstitch* the inner ring of the mouth.

7. Thread the tapestry needle with lemon yellow pearl thread. Do the whipping step of the *whipped backstitch* on the second ring (counting from the center) of the mouth.

8. Thread the chenille needle with dark olive green pearl thread. *Backstitch* the creases on the sides of the hat. *Backstitch* under the eyes and the entire nose, including the nostrils. *Backstitch* the outer ring of the mouth, the rings of the chin, the neck, and the bottom tier of the base.

9. *Backstitch* the outline of the eyes, using black pearl thread.

10. *Satin stitch* the whites of the eyes, using white pearl thread.

11. *Satin stitch* the pupils, using blue pearl thread.

You'll need

- Something to embroider
- Tools/materials for transferring the design
- Embroidery hoop, 8" (20.5 cm) diameter
- Cotton pearl thread, size 5: gold-olive, red-orange, beige-gray, lemon yellow, dark olive green, black, white, and blue
- Chenille needle, size 22
- Tapestry needle, size 22
- Embroidery scissors

Stitch Tip

This design uses lots of colors, so refer to the detail photo if you aren't sure where to stitch each color.

Dirty Martini

This is the perfect dry martini. We stitched ours onto the corner of a cocktail napkin at a "tipsy" angle. You could stitch a set of napkins in different colors to help your guests keep track of their cocktails. Or stitch a row of smaller martinis across the bottom of a bar towel.

1. Copy the pattern (page 100), and transfer it onto the fabric.

2. Put the fabric in a hoop.

3. *Backstitch* the martini glass, using dark violet pearl thread.

4. *Backstitch* the spirits, using sea green pearl thread.

5. *Backstitch* around the olives, using olive green pearl thread.

6. *Backstitch* around the pimientos, using dark plum pearl thread. Fill in the pimientos with *satin stitch*.

7. *Satin stitch* the pick, using two strands of silver floss.

You'll need

- Something to embroider
- Tools/materials for transferring the design
- Embroidery hoop, 6" (15 cm) diameter
- Chenille needle, size 22
- Cotton pearl thread, size 5: dark violet, sea green, olive green, and dark plum
- Metallic floss: silver
- Embroidery scissors

Stitch Tip

Pure cotton or linen napkins and hand towels are ideal fabrics for beginners to embroider because they are lightweight and easy to maneuver. Their moderate thread count makes it easy to stitch with pearl cotton, the best thread choice for newbies.

Royal Beast

Here's a fresh take on the traditional rearing lion often found in royal coats of arms. It's hard to believe that you can create such a dramatic and regal look with only one stitch! For added panache, we painted the inside of the lion with metallic fabric paint. If you want to embroider your lion on denim, read the tips on page 69 about stitching on denim.

1. Copy the pattern (page 100), and transfer it onto the fabric.

2. Put the fabric in a hoop, if it isn't too stiff and heavy.

3. Thread the embroidery needle with two strands of red metallic floss. *Backstitch* the entire lion.

4. Thread the tapestry needle with two strands of floss. Do the whipping step of the *whipped backstitch* on the entire lion.

5. Mix the red copper paint with the textile medium to create fabric paint, following the directions on the bottle of textile medium. Paint inside the stitching lines; carefully paint near the stitches using the spotter brush, then fill in the rest with the shader brush.

You'll need

✓ Something to embroider

✓ Tools/materials for transferring the design

✓ Embroidery hoop, 8" (20.5 cm) diameter, optional

✓ Metallic floss: red

✓ Fine crewel needle

✓ Fine tapestry needle

✓ Embroidery scissors

✓ Acrylic craft paint: metallic red copper

✓ Textile medium

✓ Fabric brushes: size 4 shader, size 5/0 spotter

Stitch Tip

It can be difficult to embroider sharp angles and tight curves. Using tiny stitches to navigate through those tight spots will give you a clear, sharp image.

Spiral (Embroidered)

A continual spiral design reflects balance, change, and harmony in life. You'd be a "zen-sation" wearing this stylized spiral in yoga class. You could also embroider it on a pillowcase, handbag, or anywhere you want to be reminded of its perspective. With our easy quilting technique and a little fabric paint, you can add a third dimension to this eternal symbol.

1. Copy the pattern (page 101), and transfer it onto the fabric.

2. Put the fabric in a hoop.

3. Cut a circle of quilt batting slightly larger than the design. Cut a circle of white cotton fabric slightly larger than the quilt batting. Center the batting under the design on the wrong side of the fabric. Center the cotton circle under the batting. Use safety pins to secure the cotton fabric and batting into position.

4. *Backstitch* the design, using variegated red pearl thread, stitching through the fabric, batting, and cotton. Begin at one of the inner points, and your stitches will bring you right back to where you started.

5. Mix the gold metallic paint with the textile medium to create fabric paint, following the directions on the bottle of textile medium. Paint inside the stitching lines; carefully paint near the stitches using the spotter brush, then fill in the rest with the shader brush.

6. Trim away the excess batting and cotton fabric from the underside of the embroidery close to the stitches. Be very careful not to snip any of your stitches.

7. Apply fabric glue to the raw edge of the cotton fabric to prevent fraying.

You'll need

- Something to embroider
- Tools/materials for transferring the design
- Embroidery hoop, 10" (25.5 cm) diameter
- Fabric shears
- Thin quilt batting
- White 100% cotton fabric
- Four large safety pins
- Cotton pearl thread, size 5: variegated red
- Chenille needle, size 22
- Embroidery scissors
- Acrylic craft paint: metallic pale gold
- Textile medium
- Fabric brushes: size 4 shader, size 5/0 spotter
- Fabric glue

Spiral (Appliqué)

Here's a variation of the spiral design used as an appliqué. It's an example of how you can be creative by changing the size and using different materials, stitches, and colors. Using this technique, you can put an embroidered embellishment on anything from a too-thick-to stitch pocket to a flower pot.

1. Copy the pattern (page 101), and transfer it onto a felt square.

2. Cut an 8" (20.5 cm) square of fusible adhesive, and fuse it to the opposite side of the felt square, following the manufacturer's instructions. Let it cool.

3. Cut out the design. Remove the paper backing, and place the design right side up in the center of the other felt square. Fuse it in place.

4. Put the felt square in a hoop.

5. *Blanket stitch* around the design, using two strands of gold metallic floss.

6. Remove the felt from the hoop. Carefully trim away the excess fabric from the design, cutting close to the stitches.

7. Lay your item flat. Apply the appliqué to your item, using fabric glue. Let the appliqué lie flat in place until the glue has dried completely.

You'll need

- Tools/materials for transferring the design
- Two 8" (20.5 cm) squares of felted wool
- Fabric shears
- Lightweight paper-backed fusible adhesive sheet
- Iron
- Embroidery hoop, 6" (15 cm) diameter
- Metallic floss: gold
- Medium crewel needle
- Embroidery scissors
- Fabric glue
- Something to embellish

Stitch Tip

If you accidentally clip a thread, use a tiny drop of fabric glue to secure it in place.

Sizzling Serpent

This dazzling reptile is very "south of the border." He can spice up a tote or beach bag, or turn up the heat on a tablecloth for a fiesta. He'd also look very hot slithering over the shoulder of a shirt. We have used the design as an appliqué, but you can stitch it directly onto your fabric.

1. Copy the pattern (page 101). Transfer the six sections of the snake pattern onto the felt pieces, and carefully cut them out.

2. Put a piece of scrap paper on the ironing board (to keep it clean) and assemble the snake pieces, facedown, on top of the paper.

3. Cut a 9" × 4" (23 × 10 cm) piece of the fusible adhesive and place it over the snake, fusible side down. Put another piece of scrap paper over the layers and fuse for 5 to 8 seconds with the iron on "wool" setting. Allow it to cool.

4. Peel the layers apart. Don't worry about being gentle... you're going to have to rip the paper. Some excess fusible adhesive will also be sticking over the edges of the felt snake; just trim that off with craft scissors.

5. Put the square of red fabric on the ironing board. Remove the paper backing from the fusible adhesive and place the snake faceup in the center of the red fabric.

6. Put the cotton scrap over the snake and mist it with water from a spray bottle. Press the iron down firmly for about 15 seconds. Allow it to cool.

7. Put the red fabric in a hoop. Thread the chenille needle with lemon yellow pearl thread. *Blanket stitch* around the snake's body. Make your stitches smaller around the head and the tip of the tail. You might have to readjust the fabric in the embroidery hoop as you go, since the snake is so long.

8. Stitch a staggered *satin stitch* along each seam between sections of the snake, using green pearl thread. This stitch is like a normal satin stitch, but the alternating stitches extend out a little on each side.

9. Remove the snake from the embroidery hoop and cut it out, leaving 1/4" (6 mm) of red fabric around its body.

10. Using the beading needle and two strands of light orange embroidery floss, attach the 22 topaz beads all over the snake. Refer to the directions for attaching single beads on page 94.

11. Attach the eye bead, using two strands of black floss.

12. Brush fabric glue onto the back of the appliqué. Stick the appliqué to the fabric item. Let the appliqué lie flat in place until the glue has dried completely.

13. Transfer the tongue pattern onto your design. Attach the seed beads, following the directions for stitching beads in a row on page 94.

You'll need

- Something to embroider
- Tools/materials for transferring the design
- Hand-dyed felt: green, blue, red, yellow, and orange
- Fabric shears
- Two 12" (30.5 cm) square pieces of paper
- Lightweight paper-backed fusible adhesive sheet
- Iron
- Craft scissors
- 12" (30.5 cm) square of red cotton fabric
- Pressing cloth (scrap of cotton fabric)
- Spray bottle and water
- Embroidery hoop, 8" (20.5 cm) diameter
- Chenille needle, size 22
- Cotton pearl thread, size 5: lemon yellow and green
- Beading needle
- Embroidery floss: light orange and black
- 22 topaz faceted beads, 4 mm
- One black/green bead, 4 mm
- One package black/green seed beads for tongue
- Embroidery scissors
- Fabric brush, size 6 shader
- Fabric glue

Bo Ho Beaded Border

Style an artsy blouse with this simple beaded border. Clothes with flat-felled seams (two stitching lines about ¼" [6mm] apart) work well for this border. The stitching lines of the seams serve as a guide for the length of the stitches. Add as many or as few beads as you like. Notice we didn't put beads under the armpits where they would rub.

1. Thread the chenille needle with blue pearl thread, and knot the end. Bring the thread to the front on one stitching line of the seam, in preparation for a *knotted blanket stitch*.

2. Slide a bead onto the thread.

3. Complete the *knotted blanket stitch*, spanning the width of the seam.

4. Continue stitching *knotted blanket stitches*, adding beads to every stitch, every other stitch, or as often as you like.

You'll need

✔ Something to embroider

✔ Cotton pearl thread, size 5: navy blue

✔ Blue, silver-lined, seed beads, size 6/0

✔ Gold, silver-lined, seed beads, size 6/0

✔ Chenille needle, size 22

✔ Embroidery scissors

Stitch Tip

Make your stitches snug to the fabric; if they're too tight, the fabric will pucker, if they're too loose, you'll have loopy threads that could get snagged. If keeping consistent tension is difficult for you, use an embroidery hoop.

Baroque Cross

Charms are uber trendy, but this baroque cross is a timeless icon. The design was stitched on craft foam. You'll be amazed how easy it is to stitch through the foam—and impressed that it looks like leather. Hang the cross on a bag, key chain, or a belt loop on jeans. You can also work the design on Ultrasuede or real leather, or stitch it directly on a shirt.

1. Copy the pattern (page 102), and transfer it onto the square of tan craft foam.

2. *Backstitch* the entire outline, using two strands of brown metallic floss.

3. *Satin stitch* the four center triangular areas, using dark brown pearl thread.

4. Squeeze a dollop of glue onto a piece of scrap paper. Then, using the tweezers, dip the back of each rhinestone into the glue and apply it to the cross. Don't worry if a tiny bit of glue shows around the edges; it dries clear.

5. Once the glue is completely dry, carefully cut out the cross, leaving a 1/8" (3 mm) border around the stitches. The smaller the scissors, the easier it is to cut.

6. Spread glue on the back of the cross, using a fabric brush. Then stick it down on the brown felt square. Let it dry.

7. Trim off the brown felt 1/8" (3 mm) beyond the foam.

8. Poke a hole through one end of the cross, using a paper piercer. Slide the small silver jump ring through the hole. Squeeze the jump ring closed, using pliers.

Stitch Tip

If you see tan craft foam peeking through the satin stitches, you can touch up little spots with an ultrafine-point permanent marker.

You'll need

- Tools/materials for transferring the design
- 3 1/2" (9 cm) square of tan craft foam
- Metallic floss: brown
- Cotton pearl thread, size 5: dark brown
- Chenille needle, size 22
- Embroidery scissors
- Jewel glue
- Scrap of paper
- Tweezers
- Rhinestones: 16 orange, 16 purple, 17 clear
- 3 1/2" (9 cm) square of brown felt
- Craft scissors
- Fabric shears
- Fabric brush, size 6 shader
- Paper piercer
- Small silver jump ring
- Pliers

Ankh Amulet

The ankh symbol is the ancient Egyptian hieroglyph representing "to live" and "everlasting life." You can create this spectacular hanging charm or stitch the design directly onto something. You could also enlarge the pattern, embroider the outline, and fill in the design with fabric paint. We suspended the ankh over the heart from a golden stitched chain. In the directions, the ankh is satin stitched, but you could use padded satin stitches to make it a little puffier.

1. Copy the pattern (page 102), and transfer it onto the center of the felt square.

2. Put the felt in a hoop.

3. Thread the chenille needle with a 20" (51 cm) length of the metallic pearl thread and knot the end. This will be your laid thread. Thread the crewel needle with one strand of gold floss. This will be your couching thread.

4. Insert the chenille needle from the back of the felt into the bottom point of the teardrop shape in the center of the ankh. Loop the laid thread over the outline, and insert the needle back through the same point. *Couch* the gold metallic pearl thread onto the teardrop outline in the center of the ankh.

5. *Couch* the top curve of the ankh, the bottom post, the left arm, and then the right arm, continuously.

6. End the laid thread by making one long straight stitch down the center of the bottom post. Cut the thread close to the fabric.

7. *Couch* over the entire laid thread again, spacing the stitches close together. End the couching thread on the back side.

8. *Satin stitch* the ankh from the bottom up around the curve, using gold metallic pearl thread. Keep the stitches perpendicular to the sides as you round the curve.

9. *Satin stitch* the arms.

10. Remove the felt from the hoop. Trim away excess fabric from the design, carefully cutting close to the stitches.

11. If you want to make the amulet look as if it is hanging from a necklace, *chain stitch* a faux necklace along the front edge of a tank top or T-shirt.

12. Thread the beading needle with one strand of gold metallic floss; double it and knot the ends. Secure it to the top, back of the amulet. String several beads onto the floss and then secure it to the bottom of the chain-stitched necklace. Add a dot of fabric glue at both attachment points for added security.

You'll need

✔ Tools/materials for transferring the design

✔ 5" (12.7 cm) square of yellow or gold felted wool

✔ Embroidery hoop, 4" (10 cm) diameter

✔ Chenille needle, size 22

✔ Cotton pearl thread, size 5: gold metallic

✔ Medium crewel needle

✔ Metallic floss: gold

✔ Two safety pins

✔ Embroidery scissors

✔ Beading needle

✔ Fabric glue

✔ Gold glass seed beads or beads of your choice

Stitch Tip

When you are couching, insert a safety pin into your fabric off to the side, and wrap the laid thread around it to keep it out of your way. Use the same technique to keep the couching thread out of the way while you prepare the next section of the laid thread.

Dress Like an Egyptian

This band of gold with touches of turquoise and coral was inspired by the fascinating and priceless "collar" adornments of the ancient Egyptians. Choose a top with a large enough neckline to go over your head without stretching, because the embroidered embellishment will not stretch. Pick gold trims that are all the same color; some are more yellow or brassy than others.

1. Mark a line 2" (5 cm) below the edge of the neckline, using a light-colored transfer pen or pencil.

2. *Chain stitch* the marked line, using turquoise pearl thread.

3. *Couch* a band of the ¼" (6 mm) gold braid above and below the turquoise chain stitching, using one strand of gold metallic floss. Join the ends of the trims at a shoulder seam or in the center of the back, to make them less visible.

4. Pin the fancy gold trim directly above the top gold braid with safety pins. Fill in every other space in the center of the trim with a few *straight stitches*, using the coral pearl thread. Remove the safety pins as you come to them.

5. Thread the beading needle with one strand of gold floss. Attach a gold seed bead in the open spaces in the center of the trim.

6. Thread the chenille needle with the gold metallic pearl thread (remember, you don't separate pearl threads). *Couch* a gold elastic thread just above the fancy trim, catching some loops of the trim in the stitches.

7. *Couch* another gold elastic cord just above the first one, stitching over both cords.

8. Thread the beading needle with one strand of gold floss. Attach the gold and black bugle beads over the turquoise chain stitching and gold braids. Use the seed beads and coral stitches as a guide for spacing the bugle beads. (See photo.)

9. Stitch a gold seed bead at the lower edge of the trim, even with each bugle bead.

10. Metallic threads can be itchy. Finish by sewing a soft ribbon or seam binding over the exposed threads on the inside of the top.

Stitch Tip

Trims and cording will unravel when they are cut. To prevent this, brush the spot where you'll be cutting with fabric or jewel glue. Let the glue dry completely, then cut. No frayed ends!

You'll need

- ✔ Something to embroider
- ✔ Transfer pen or pencil
- ✔ Tape measure
- ✔ Cotton pearl thread, size 5: turquoise and coral
- ✔ Chenille needle, size 22
- ✔ Embroidery scissors
- ✔ Gold braid, 1/4" (6 mm) wide, enough to go around the neck-line twice plus 6" (15 cm)
- ✔ Metallic floss: gold
- ✔ Gold glass seed beads, size 10/0
- ✔ Gold elastic cord, 5 mm, enough to go around the neck-line twice plus 6" (15 cm)
- ✔ Metallic pearl thread, size 5: gold
- ✔ Craft scissors or shears
- ✔ Four safety pins
- ✔ Fancy gold trim, enough to go around the neckline once plus 3" (7.5 cm)
- ✔ Beading needle
- ✔ Gold bugle beads, 1/2" (1.3 cm) long
- ✔ Black bugle beads, 1/4" (6 mm) long
- ✔ Ribbon or seam binding
- ✔ General sewing thread in color to match garment
- ✔ General sewing needle

Butterflies

Wouldn't these spa slippers be an adorable baby shower gift for a mom-to-be? Stitch them in pink, blue, yellow, or a rainbow! A photo album cover with a butterfly to represent each grandchild would also be a precious gift for a grandmother. The directions take you through one butterfly with two-tone wings.

1. Draw a line ½" to ¾" (1.3 to 2 cm) long with the transfer pen or pencil where you'd like the butterfly to rest.

2. Thread the chenille needle with the color of pearl thread that you want for the head and forewings, and make a tight little knot at the end.

3. Insert the needle at the head of the marked line and bring it out at a point slightly lower on the line where you'd like the forewing to be.

4. Loop the pearl thread around your fingertip. Insert the needle back into the fabric just below where it came out. Don't pull the pearl thread tight; leave the loop hanging free while you push the needle through directly across from the first wing stitch. Repeat to make a wing opposite the first one.

5. Repeat step 4 to create the desired number of loops for the forewings, making the same number of loops (1 to 3) on each side of the line.

6. Bring the needle out on the line, and snip the thread, leaving a little nub hanging. (You'll anchor this thread with jewel glue later.)

7. Thread the chenille needle with the second color of pearl thread and knot the end. Insert the needle at the bottom of the line and bring the needle out just below the forewings.

8. Repeat steps 4 and 5 to make hindwings. You can adjust the size of the loopy wings by very gently pulling them a tiny bit in either direction.

9. Put a drop of jewel glue on your fingertip and run it across the underside of each wing that you'd like to lie flat. Arrange the wings and press gently to secure them into place.

10. Snip off the bottom knot and place a small dot of glue over the spot to secure the remaining bit of thread. Let the glue dry.

11. Thread the beading needle with one strand of white pearlescent floss; knot the end. Insert the needle midway along the transfer line, and bring it out at the top of the line.

12. Stitch two 10/0 seed beads slightly above the head for the antennae.

13. Bring the needle out right under the knot head. String on the larger 6/0 seed beads to cover the length of the line, including the spot where you snipped off the knot in step 6. Insert the needle into the fabric at the bottom end of the transfer line. Then *couch* the beads in place, taking a stitch after each bead.

14. Stitch two or three tiny stitches over the wing loops that you glued down in step 9, using the same pearlescent floss.

15. Bring the needle out at the top of head. Tie a tiny tight knot and clip the thread close to the knot. Put a tiny drop of jewel glue on the knot to secure it.

You'll need

✔ Something to embroider

✔ Transfer pencil or pen

✔ Chenille needle, size 22

✔ Cotton pearl thread, size 5: light green, medium blue, light blue, light cranberry, light violet, and yellow

✔ Embroidery scissors

✔ Jewel glue

✔ Beading needle

✔ Pearlescent floss: white

✔ Two seed beads, size 10/0 for each butterfly in color to match threads

✔ Four to six seed beads, size 6/0 for each butterfly in color to match threads

Time Flies

Time does fly, but this design reminds us all to take some time for ourselves. We used tranquil colors of cotton pearl thread and beads to stitch our winged clock on this spa mask. You could make your statement in brighter colors, if you wish.

1. Copy the pattern (page 102), and transfer it onto the fabric. Transfer just the clock face onto the blue fabric.

2. Apply paper-backed fusible adhesive to the wrong side of the blue fabric, following the manufacturer's directions. Let it cool.

3. Cut out the clock face. Remove the paper backing and fuse the clock face to the center of the design.

4. Put the fabric in a hoop. Thread the chenille needle with yellow cotton pearl thread. *Chain stitch* the inner ring of the clock face, using yellow cotton pearl thread.

5. Attach the four 6/0 seed beads with a little droplet of jewel glue, putting a bead at 12:00, 3:00, 6:00, and 9:00. Place them with the holes parallel to the circle so you can stitch through them later. This will keep the large beads in the right places when you add the smaller seed beads. Let the glue dry.

6. Thread the beading needle with one strand of medium blue embroidery floss. Knot the end and bring the thread up next to one of the large beads. Slip the needle through the large bead. Then string small beads onto the thread until you have a comfortable fit between two of the large 6/0 seed beads. Glue the small beads in place.

7. Continue adding small seed beads around the clock.

8. Thread the crewel needle with two strands of medium lavender embroidery floss. *Straight stitch* the Roman numerals on the clock. *Whip* over the stitches to make them more visible.

9. *Backstitch* the wings, using two strands of very light blue pearlescent floss and one strand of very light blue cotton floss blended together. See page 78 for directions on blending threads.

You'll need

✔ Something to embroider

✔ Tools/materials for transferring the design

✔ Light blue cotton fabric, about 2" (5 cm) square

✔ Paper-backed fusible adhesive sheet

✔ Iron

✔ Embroidery hoop

✔ Embroidery scissors

✔ Chenille needle, size 22

✔ Cotton pearl thread, size 5: yellow

✔ Four turquoise seed beads, size 6/0

✔ Jewel glue

✔ Beading needle

✔ Medium crewel needle

✔ Cotton embroidery floss: medium blue, medium lavender, and very light blue

✔ One package turquoise seed beads, size 10/0

✔ Pearlescent embroidery floss: very light blue

Crown Jewels

A cool grandmother asked us for a sparkly craft project that she could make with her tween-aged granddaughters. This imperial crown design turned out to be just the thing. We stitched it on the back of a terry robe. Simply stitch the outline and then embellish the crown with your favorite bling: sequins, beads, craft gems, fancy buttons, costume jewelry, even glittering dimensional fabric paints.

1. Copy the pattern (page 103), and transfer it onto the fabric.

2. Put the fabric in a hoop.

3. *Chain stitch* the top points of the crown, using lemon yellow pearl thread.

4. *Chain stitch* the scallop above the base and the two side hearts on the center point, using light cranberry pearl thread.

5. *Chain stitch* the base of the crown, using medium blue pearl thread.

6. *Chain stitch* the two large hearts on the center point, using ruby pearl thread.

7. Now the fun begins! Assemble your gems and rhinestones. Lay them out on the crown and try some different arrangements. When you decide on the perfect look, glue all of the sparkly stuff in place with jewel glue. Let the glue dry completely before you parade around in your regalia.

You'll need

✔ Something to embroider

✔ Tools/materials for transferring the design

✔ Embroidery hoop

✔ Cotton pearl thread, size 5: lemon yellow, light cranberry, ruby, and medium blue

✔ Chenille needle, size 22

✔ Embroidery scissors

✔ Jewel glue

✔ Plastic craft gems

✔ Rhinestones

Stitch Tip

If you want to embroider on terry cloth, it will be easier if you spray-starch and iron the area before applying the design. This will flatten the pile and make it easier to stitch. It will fluff back up when you wash it.

Steamy

This design is a combination of embroidery, appliqué, and bead-work. It looks complicated, but the stitches are easy. The cup looks just right on a placemat, a tea towel, or a napkin. For a perfect hostess gift, line a basket with your embroidery and fill it with tea or coffee and some sweets.

1. Copy the pattern (page 104), and transfer it onto the floral fabric. Cut it out, using fabric shears.

2. Dip the fabric brush into fabric glue and apply a thin layer to the back of the floral fabric cutout. The glue dries quickly, so work fast. Flip the cutout over and stick it to the item to be embroidered. Let it dry.

3. Working one small area at a time, squeeze a thin line of fabric glue along the edges of the pattern and carefully lay the dark pearl thread onto the glue, as an outline. Let it dry.

4. Thread a general sewing needle with one strand of dark embroidery floss. *Couch* over the pearl thread.

5. Run a thin line of fabric glue directly under the rim of the teacup and the rim of the saucer. Lay a piece of gold metallic ribbon over that, flush with the embroidery floss. Then, squeeze another thin line of glue about ¹/₄" (6 mm) under the rim of the cup and repeat. Let dry completely.

6. Thread the general sewing needle with one strand of gold metallic floss. *Couch* over the gold metallic ribbon.

7. Thread the chenille needle with four strands of gold metallic floss. Satin stitch the teacup handle.

8. Realign the pattern over the design and transfer the dots for the beads.

9. Thread the beading needle with one strand of pearlescent embroidery floss. Attach the beads, using the method for attaching single beads on page 94. Use one continuous thread for each curl of steam.

You'll need

✔ Something to embroider

✔ Tools/materials for transferring the design

✔ 100% cotton floral fabric

✔ Fabric shears

✔ Fabric glue

✔ Fabric brush, size 4 shader

✔ Cotton pearl thread, size 5, in dark color to coordinate with fabric

✔ General sewing needle

✔ Embroidery floss in same color as pearl thread

✔ ¹/₁₆" (1.5 mm) gold metallic ribbon

✔ Embroidery scissors

✔ Embroidery floss: gold metallic and pearlescent

✔ Chenille needle, size 22

✔ Beading needle

✔ Pearlescent seed beads

Crabby

This design combines a few simple stitches with a very easy appliqué. It would be oh-so-cute on baby items like this onesie, or on a bath or beach towel. You could also make a statement about somebody's crabby moments on a scrapbook page or card. On any baby item, avoid any risk of choking by using French knots for the eyes instead of beads.

1. Copy the pattern (page 102), and transfer the whole crab design to the garment. Transfer the body and snapper designs to the flannel.

2. Put the flannel in a hoop. *Double running stitch* the mouth, using two strands of cranberry floss. Remove the flannel from the hoop.

3. Cut out the body and snappers. Evenly spread a tiny amount of fabric glue on the back of the body. (This will keep the edges from fraying and will keep the pieces in place during stitching.) Before the glue begins to dry, quickly stick the body to the garment. Repeat with each snapper.

4. Center the design in an embroidery hoop. *Blanket stitch* around the body, using two strands of lavender floss; stitch through the flannel and the garment.

5. *Blanket stitch* around the snappers, using two strands of yellow-green floss.

6. Stitch the legs, using two strands of lavender floss. The legs on the onesie were done in *whipped backstitch*. For quicker and easier legs, use a *basic back-stitch, stem stitch, split stitch,* or *chain stitch.* The best choice for paper crafting would be *double running stitch.*

7. Make the eyes with *French knots,* using six strands of black floss. If your project is not a baby item, sew on black beads for the eyes, using two strands of black floss.

Stitch Tip

Keep your stitches in scale with the design and with what you're stitching on. Use little stitches on tiny baby things and bigger stitches on larger items.

You'll need

✓ Something to embroider

✓ Flannel fabric, about 6" × 6" (15 × 15 cm)

✓ Tools/materials for transferring design

✓ Embroidery hoop, 4" (10 cm) diameter

✓ Fine crewel needle

✓ Cotton embroidery floss: light cranberry, lavender, yellow-green, and black

✓ Fabric shears

✓ Fabric glue

✓ Two black 6/0 seed beads (optional)

Happy Herbivore

Our spunky niece Kyla is absolutely crazy about dinosaurs. We thought that any child who plays "food chain" instead of dolls was in desperate need of cute dinosaur garb. Stitch this friendly dino on anything in any colors.

1. Copy the pattern (102), and transfer it onto the fabric.

2. *Blanket stitch* from the nape of the dinosaur's neck to his rump, using two strands of fluorescent green embroidery floss.

3. Continue to *blanket stitch* down the top of the dinosaur's tail, but flip the stitch in the other direction. Stop at the tip.

4. *Backstitch* the rest of the design.

5. Give your dinosaur two "beady" eyes, following the directions for attaching single beads on page 94. If the item you are stitching is going to be within a baby's reach, substitute *French knots* stitched with three strands of green embroidery floss.

You'll need

✔ Something to embroider

✔ Tools/materials for transferring the design

✔ Fine crewel needle

✔ Embroidery floss: fluorescent green

✔ Embroidery scissors

✔ Beading needle

✔ Two teal seed beads

Team Spirit "10"

This is a great design for a little sport or for the jock in your life. Customize it with team colors. You could stitch just the number "1" to let everybody know who's your number one. We're showing you how to use the design one way on the front, another way on the back. Go ahead and substitute your favorite stitches.

STITCHES ONLY

1. Copy the pattern (page 108), and transfer the entire design onto the fabric. Draw a 5½" (14 cm) circle around the numbers.

2. Put the fabric in a hoop.

3. Thread the chenille needle with beige-gray pearl thread. *Running stitch* the numbers.

4. Thread the tapestry needle with beige-gray pearl thread. Do the whipping step of the *whipped running stitch* on the numbers.

5. *Running stitch* the outline around the numbers, using dark navy blue pearl thread.

6. Stitch the circle with *whipped running stitch*, using dark red pearl thread for both steps.

WITH PAINT

1. Copy the pattern (page 108), and transfer the design onto the fabric, omitting the outline. Draw a 4" (10 cm) circle around the numbers.

2. Put the fabric in a hoop.

3. Thread the chenille needle with dark navy blue pearl thread. *Running stitch* the numbers.

4. Thread the tapestry needle with dark navy blue pearl thread. Do the whipping step of the *whipped running stitch* on the numbers.

5. *Running stitch* the circle, using dark navy blue pearl thread.

6. Mix the ivory paint with the textile medium to create fabric paint, following the directions on the bottle of textile medium. Paint inside the stitching lines of the numbers; carefully paint near the stitches using the spotter brush, then fill in the rest with the shader brush. The numbers will have a cool, retro look if your painting job is a bit untidy, but don't paint on your stitches.

You'll need

✓ Something to embroider

✓ Tools/materials for transferring the design

✓ Embroidery hoop, 6" (15 cm) diameter

✓ Cotton pearl thread, size 5: dark navy blue, dark red, beige-gray

✓ Chenille needle, size 22

✓ Tapestry needle, size 22

✓ Embroidery scissors

✓ Acrylic craft paint: ivory

✓ Textile medium

✓ Fabric brushes: size 4 shader and size 5/0 spotter

Stitch Tip

Add a circle around any design by tracing the outline of a cup or an embroidery hoop or anything around the house that's the right size for your design. You can also use a compass, if you have one handy.

Almost Argyle

You could, of course, use this animated argyle design for almost anything, but we used it to make a campy tote, so we've included directions for decorating the handles. Being Illini fans, we naturally made it orange and blue! Use your team colors, or try one of these fabulous combos: red/royal purple, pink/lavender, coral/kiwi, sky blue/violet, burgundy/navy, raspberry/tangerine, eggplant/lemon, key lime/lemon, or the ever-popular pink/black.

ARGYLE PATTERN

I. Copy the pattern (page 105) and transfer it, including the stitching lines, onto the felt.

2. Fuse the fusible adhesive to the opposite side of the felt, following the manufacturer's instructions. Let it cool.

3. Cut out the shapes.

4. Transfer the pattern onto the canvas bag. Remove the paper backing from the shapes, and place them right side up on the bag. Fuse them in place.

5. *Running stitch* the center diamond, using light tan pearl thread.

6. *Double running stitch* the remaining design lines, first using orange and then royal blue pearl thread.

HANDLES

I. Measure the handles. Add ½" (1.3 cm) to the width and 1" (2.5 cm) to the length measurements. Draw these measurements onto the felt, making two strips of each color. Cut them out.

2. Apply a line of glue to one side of a handle. Spread the glue out along the handle. Adhere a felt strip to the handle, letting the felt overlap the edges ¼" (6 mm). Repeat for both sides of each handle.

3. *Blanket stitch* both long edges of each handle, using light tan pearl thread.

4. Trim the front and back strips of felt at the ends of both handles. Secure the ends with stitches or fabric glue.

You'll need

✔ Something to embroider

✔ Tools/materials for transferring the design

✔ Orange and blue craft felt

✔ Paper-backed fusible adhesive sheet

✔ Iron

✔ Fabric shears

✔ Cotton pearl thread, size 5: light tan, orange, and royal blue

✔ Chenille needle, size 22

✔ Embroidery scissors

✔ Tape measure

✔ Fabric glue

✔ Craft scissors or shears

Love

The Chinese character for "love" makes a striking design for embroidery. We embellished a large bolster pillow, first stenciling and then stitching the design. Slightly offsetting the stitches from the stencil gives the design depth. You can achieve this impressive effect with only one color of paint, one strand of pearl thread, and one easy stitch.

1. Copy the pattern (page 105), and transfer it onto cardstock. Place the cardstock on a self-healing cutting mat and cut out the design areas, using a craft knife. This will be used as a stencil.

2. Mix the white paint with the textile medium to create fabric paint, following the directions on the bottle of textile medium. It's okay, even desirable, if the paint seems a little watered down.

3. Place the stencil on the fabric and secure the edges with tape. Place a piece of scrap paper under the fabric to keep the paint from bleeding through.

4. Paint in the stencil, using the fabric brush and working from the outside of each area in.

5. Remove the stencil and let the paint dry for several hours.

6. Transfer the pattern onto the fabric about 1/8" (3 mm) askew from the painted character.

7. Put the fabric in a hoop. *Backstitch* the entire outline of the design, using variegated blue pearl thread.

You'll need

✔ Something to embroider

✔ Tools/materials for transferring the design

✔ Scrap of cardstock

✔ Self-healing cutting mat

✔ Craft knife

✔ Acrylic craft paint: white

✔ Textile medium

✔ Tape

✔ Fabric brush: size 4 shader

✔ Embroidery hoop, 8" (20.5 cm) diameter

✔ Chenille needle, size 22

✔ Cotton pearl thread, size 5: variegated blue

✔ Embroidery scissors

Sweet Confection

Dainty and delectable, this embroidered border was just the thing to accent the neckline of a plain white sweater. The design has three pretty elements: a pink square chain stitch, a sky blue coral stitch, and a scattering of beads. Choose one, two, or use all three.

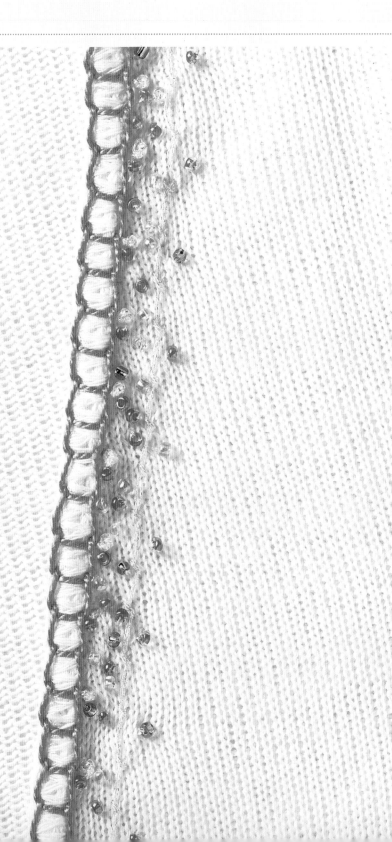

1. Thread the chenille needle with pink pearl thread. *Square chain stitch* the edge of the neckline.

2. Thread the chenille needle with all six strands of white pearlescent floss. Make *French knots* next to the square chain stitches, using the chain-stitch "rungs" as a guide for spacing.

3. Thread the crewel needle with three strands of sky blue pearlescent floss. *Coral stitch* a line 1/4" (6 mm) from the square chain stitching.

4. Thread the beading needle with a single strand of white pearlescent floss. Sew on seed beads randomly along both sides of the coral stitching. Refer to the directions for attaching single beads on page 94.

You'll need

- Something to embroider
- Chenille needle, size 22
- Cotton pearl thread, size 5: pink
- Embroidery scissors
- Pearlescent embroidery floss: sky blue and white
- Fine crewel needle
- Beading needle
- Seed beads, size 10/0: clear ultraluscent, pink, and light blue turquoise

Wedding Keepsake

Embroidery and beading have been part of bridal gowns and accessories for generations. These embellishments will turn a linen and lace handkerchief into a keepsake for a bride. The petite organza ribbon bouquet in one corner has a crystal heart and a tiny ivory star for love and luck. A single blue crystal bead is "something blue." This delicate delight does take some time, but it's not difficult and it will be treasured forever.

RIBBON BORDER

1. Secure the satin ribbon along the edge of the linen, using small safety pins.

2. Mark a dot every ¼" (6 mm) along the inner edge of the ribbon with a transfer pen or pencil.

3. *Square chain stitch* over the ribbon, using two strands of white pearlescent floss. Use the marked dots as a guide for stitch placement.

4. Thread the beading needle with one strand of white pearlescent floss and stitch the mini beads along the inner edge of the ribbon on the linen. Attach each bead even with the side of a stitch. We used alternating pearl and lavender colored mini beads.

PETITE RIBBON BOUQUET

1. Tie the organza ribbon into a bow. Stitch it to a corner of the linen, using white pearlescent floss.

2. Cut several pieces of fishing line with different lengths, from 1½" to 3" (3.8 to 7.5 cm).

3. Dip one end of the fishing line into the jewel glue. Add beads, crystals, or charms from the opposite end, sliding them down onto the glue to secure them into place.

4. Dip the other end of the fishing line into the jewel glue and slide some beads toward this end as well. Let the beaded fishing line pieces dry.

5. Add a large drop of jewel glue to the center of the bow. Place the beaded fishing line pieces onto the glue, radiating in different directions. (See photo.)

6. Place additional beads/crystals onto the wet glue to cover the ends of the fishing line. Let the glue dry completely.

EMBELLISHED LACE

1. Thread the beading needle with one strand of white pearlescent floss. Sew ultraluscent beads onto the lace, weaving the floss through the lace to attach single beads and clusters of three to five beads throughout the lace. Place beads into the lace patterns (like flower centers) and/or randomly throughout the lace. Make sure to keep your floss tension even (but not tight); you really don't want the handkerchief to pucker up!

2. Knot the back of each single bead or cluster of beads as you add them. If you're willing to spend more time beading, you can add beads to the back side of the handkerchief as well.

3. When you've finished attaching beads to the lace, turn the handkerchief over and place a tiny dot of jewel glue on each knot to secure them.

You'll need

✔ Item to be embroidered

✔ Satin ribbon, ⅛" (3 mm) wide, enough to outline the linen center of the handkerchief

✔ Safety pins

✔ Ruler or tape measure

✔ Transfer pen or pencil

✔ Fine crewel needle

✔ Pearlescent pearl thread, size 5: white

✔ Embroidery scissors

✔ Beading needle

✔ Mini seed beads: pearl and lavender

✔ ½ yd. (0.5 m) organza ribbon, ½" (12 mm) wide

✔ Clear fishing line

✔ Jewel glue

✔ Seed beads, size 10/0: utraluscent and pink

✔ Crystal heart

✔ Embellishments and charms of choice

✔ Craft scissors or shears

Stitch Tip

Make a luxurious ring bearer's pillow by sewing a second identical handkerchief to the back of the embroidered one and stuffing it.

Eiffel Tower

This whimsical design is perfect for a travel journal, scrapbook page, or bon voyage card. Here we used the design to create a monumentally sentimental box to hold travel mementos. We stitched on fabric from a friend's dress shirt that had lived its days—the button was from the cuff. You can use a standard cigar box or buy a box from a craft store. The design was stitched in romantic, softly colored linen floss.

1. Copy the pattern (page 106), and transfer it onto the fabric.

2. Put the fabric in a hoop.

3. *Backstitch* the lower curve and vertical lines of the Eiffel Tower, using three strands of light blue floss.

4. *Backstitch* the horizontal lines of the tower, using three strands of tan floss.

5. *Backstitch* the crossed lines in the center of the design, using three strands of light gold floss.

6. Stitch the button to the top of the tower.

7. *Cross-stitch* around the border, using three strands of pink floss.

You'll need

✔ Something to embroider

✔ Tools/materials for transferring the design

✔ Embroidery hoop, 8" (20.5 cm) diameter

✔ Linen embroidery floss: pink, light gold, light blue, and tan

✔ Medium crewel needle

✔ Embroidery scissors

✔ Small button

Stitch Tip

If you want to attach your fabric design to a wooden box, sand the box top lightly first. Then brush it with a thin layer of fabric glue and smooth the fabric in place.

Note Book

Stitch this G clef on a notebook to create a gift for someone who studies, teaches, or just loves music. The directions tell how to stitch a design on a plastic notebook cover. Add ribbons for a symphony of color. You could use black and white ribbons for pianists or silver for a flutist or gold for a horn player. Bravo!

1. Copy the pattern (page 107) and tape it to the note-book cover.

2. Put the self-healing cutting mat under the cover. Then, following the hole guides on the pattern, use the paper piercer to poke holes through the cover.

3. Thread the chenille needle with dark lavender pearl thread. *Backstitch* the outline of the clef sign.

4. Thread the tapestry needle with dark yellow pearl thread. Work the weaving step of the *double woven backstitches*. Be sure to keep the loops even on both sides.

5. Tie ribbon scraps and specialty yarns to the notebook's spiral binding.

You'll need

✓ Notebook (or folder)

✓ Tools/materials for transferring the design

✓ Tape

✓ Paper piercer

✓ Self-healing cutting mat

✓ Cotton pearl thread, size 5: dark yellow and dark lavender

✓ Chenille needle, size 22

✓ Tapestry needle, size 22

✓ Embroidery scissors

✓ Fabric shears

✓ Ribbon scraps

✓ Specialty yarn

Stitch Tip

If the notebook cover is particularly thick, you may need to use a hammer and thin nail to pierce the holes.

Celebration

Try your new stitching skills to make special cards. Check out the huge variety of amazing new decorative papers. Any papers can be used for the cupcake and candle, but be sure to use cardstock for the rectangular background. It's sturdier than ordinary thin paper, so it won't rip when you pull the stitches tight.

1. Copy the pattern (page 107). Transfer the cupcake icing and the cupcake bottom onto decorative paper. Transfer the candle onto white cardstock. You can ignore the wick and flame for now.

2. Using the craft knife and ruler, cut a 2¾" × 4¼" (7 × 10.8 cm) rectangle of decorative paper. Apply spray adhesive to the back of this rectangle and mount it onto another paper. Trim the back paper, leaving a margin of ¹/₁₆" (1.5 mm). Use a ruler and craft knife for accuracy.

3. Transfer the complete cupcake pattern onto the center of the assembled paper. This will be your guide for placement in the next step.

4. Apply spray adhesive to the back of the cupcake bottom, icing, and candle cutouts. Mount them to the panel.

5. Place the panel on the self-healing cutting mat and mouse pad. Using the paper piercer, poke holes about ⅛" (3 mm) apart on the stitching line of the cupcake icing. *Double running stitch* the cupcake icing, using lavender pearl thread. Begin and end at the candle.

6. Poke holes about ⅛" (3 mm) apart on the stitching lines of the cupcake bottom. *Double running stitch* the lines of the cupcake bottom, using yellow pearl thread.

7. Poke holes through the striped paper at the ends of the diagonal candle lines. *Straight stitch* the diagonal lines, using pink pearl thread.

8. Poke holes at the ends of the wick line. *Straight stitch* the wick, using lavender pearl thread.

9. Poke a hole at the very top point of the flame and at the bottom. Then poke four parallel holes down each side of the flame. *Straight stitch* one stitch from the top of the flame to the bottom, using yellow pearl thread. Then *straight stitch* side to side up the flame, covering the vertical stitch.

10. Poke a hole through each dot of "candle glimmer." Thread the beading needle with one strand of pearlescent floss. Bring the needle up through the first hole, string a bead, and return the needle back through the same hole. Move to the next hole and repeat. Attach all the beads with the same thread, moving from hole to hole.

11. Cut a 9" × 6" (23 × 15 cm) rectangle of decorative paper and fold it in half to create a 4½" × 6" (11.5 × 15 cm) card. (This will fit a standard-size envelope.)

12. Apply a small piece of double stick tape to the back of each corner of the embroidered panel. Stick the embroidered panel onto the center of the card front.

13. Open the card and poke holes through the card front along the edge of the panel, ½" (1.3 cm) from each corner. At each corner, stitch pink pearl thread into one hole from the front, then back up through the other hole. Slide the needle off the thread and tie a small bow. Trim the thread ends. Touch the center of each bow with a small dot of glue.

You'll need

- ✓ Decorative papers
- ✓ White cardstock
- ✓ Craft scissors
- ✓ Ruler
- ✓ Craft knife
- ✓ Spray adhesive
- ✓ Self-healing cutting mat
- ✓ Mouse pad
- ✓ Paper piercer
- ✓ Chenille needle, size 22
- ✓ Cotton pearl thread, size 5: pink, yellow, and lavender
- ✓ Embroidery scissors
- ✓ Beading needle
- ✓ Pearlescent embroidery floss
- ✓ Pearlescent seed beads
- ✓ Double stick tape
- ✓ Glue

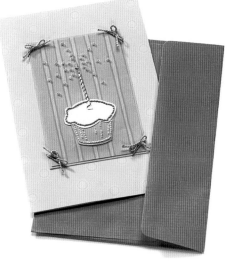

61

Party Balloon

This happy balloon design will perk up any "blah" bag. You can personalize it with writing or cut a circle from the center to insert a photo (also great for a scrapbook page!).

1. Copy the pattern (page 108). Transfer the large balloon pattern onto the white cardstock. Transfer the small balloon pattern onto the yellow paper. You can ignore the spiral and crease detail at the bottom for now. Cut along the outlines to create both balloon layers.

2. Apply spray adhesive to the back of the yellow balloon. Mount the yellow balloon onto the front of the white balloon.

3. Align the small balloon pattern over the yellow mounted balloon and transfer the spiral and crease detail onto the mounted balloon layers.

4. Place the balloon on the self-healing cutting mat and mouse pad. Using the paper piercer, poke holes about 1/4" (6 mm) apart along of the edge of the yellow balloon. Poke holes along the spiral and crease detail, spacing them about 1/8" (3 mm) apart.

5. *Double running stitch* the outline and detail lines of the balloon, using aquamarine pearl thread.

6. Place the embroidered balloon on the gift bag and mark the location of the crease detail near the bottom. Remove the balloon and cut a small slit in the bag at the mark, using a craft knife.

7. Curl lengths of ribbon by pulling them across the scissors blade. Trim them to the desired length and insert the ends through the slit. Tape the ends in place on the inside of the bag.

8. Apply foam circles to the back of the embroidered balloon and mount it onto the gift bag.

You'll need

- Gift bag or other item to be embellished
- White cardstock
- Yellow paper
- Craft knife
- Spray adhesive
- Self-healing cutting mat
- Mouse pad
- Paper piercer
- Chenille needle, size 22
- Cotton pearl thread, size 5: aquamarine
- Embroidery scissors
- Lime green and hot pink curling ribbon
- Craft scissors
- Tape
- PeelnStick foam circles

Scrapbook Frames

If you scrap, there's no limit to what you can do with thread and the designs in this book! This project and the next one are just for you. They make special frames for a page to put in a book or in a shadow box display. We've used them to honor our studio cat, Toby, who dedicated lots of time napping and sitting on all of our projects.

FRAME 1

1. Copy the pattern (page 109) for frame 1. Transfer the pattern for the paper back to decorative paper; transfer the pattern for the foam top to white craft foam. Cut them out using the craft knife and ruler.

2. Spray the back of the craft foam with adhesive and carefully center it over the paper frame. Press it down firmly.

3. If you haven't already transferred the stitch guide dots, lay the pattern back down over the foam frame. Using the dot guides and the paper piercer, poke two rows of holes for the cross-stitches. Remember to work on the self-healing cutting mat and mouse pad.

4. *Cross-stitch* the border, using pink pearl thread.

5. Pick a photo for the center of your frame. Place the frame facedown; center the photo over the opening. Secure it to the back of the frame with one side of double-sided tacky tape. Leave the paper backing on the other side of the tape for now.

FRAME 2

1. Copy the pattern (page 110) for frame 2. Transfer the pattern for the paper top to decorative paper, and cut it out using the craft knife and ruler. Don't cut the corner off of the frame yet; just transfer it as one complete rectangle. It'll save time and make the edges of your frame perfectly align.

2. Spray the back of the paper frame with adhesive and stick it over a piece of purple craft foam, leaving a little room around the edges.

3. Using the ruler and craft knife, cut out the center opening and sides of the frame, leaving 1/16" (1.5 mm) outer margin of purple foam. Cut the rectangular corner away from the frame.

4. If you haven't already done so, transfer the stitch guides onto the paper frame and use the paper piercer to poke holes 1/8" (3 mm) apart.

5. *Straight stitch* through the holes, using white pearl thread.

6. Attach the photo, as in step 5 above. Use the craft knife and a ruler to cut the upper left corner off your photo, following the guidelines on the pattern.

7. To attach the frames, place double-sided tacky tape down along the bottom right corner of frame 1, following the pattern guide. Press the two pieces of frame 2 down as close as possible to the white foam border.

8. Remove the paper backing from the tape on the backs of the interlocking frames. Add more pieces of tape, if necessary, and stick the frames to your scrapbook page.

You'll need

✔ Decorative papers

✔ Light blue cardstock

✔ White craft foam

✔ Purple craft foam

✔ Craft knife

✔ Ruler

✔ Spray adhesive

✔ Chenille needle, size 22

✔ Paper piercer

✔ Self-healing cutting mat

✔ Mouse pad

✔ Cotton pearl thread, size 5: pink and white

✔ Double-sided tacky tape

Scrapbook Pocket

We created a layered and stitched craft foam pocket to cradle a framed photo. Embroidery is a great way to set off the title and edges of your scrapbook page, too. We used two strands of floss to double running stitch close to the letters. The second row is double running stitch in pearl thread, whipped with a single strand of floss. The outer border is whipped running stitch in pearl thread. To hide thread ends and stitching, we backed the whole page with another page and blanket stitched the outer edges.

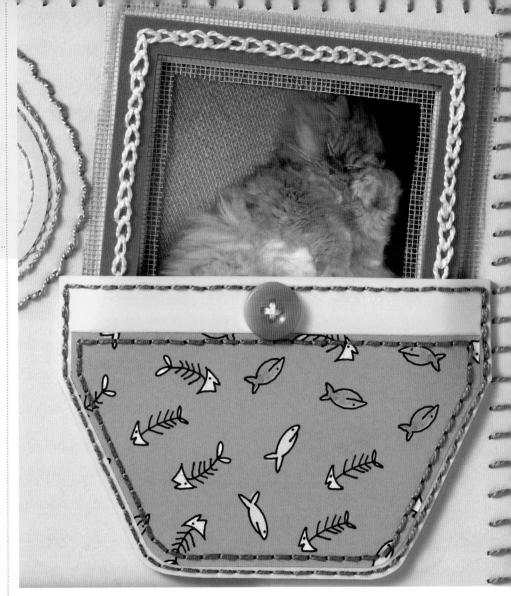

FRAME

1. Copy the pattern (page 110). Transfer the pattern for the foam top to blue craft foam. Transfer the pattern for the cardstock back onto yellow cardstock. Transfer the pattern for the mesh middle to tangerine mesh. Cut them out using the craft knife and ruler.

2. Cut four ⅛" (3 mm) squares of double-sided tacky tape and stick them to the back outer corners of the blue craft foam frame. Remove the paper backing, center the blue frame over the mesh frame, and press it down. Then, flip the whole thing over, cut four more small squares of tape, and place them over the first ones.

3. Remove the paper backing from the tape. Center the mesh and foam frame over the yellow frame, and press it down.

4. Place the pattern on top of the assembled frames and use the dot guides and the paper piercer to poke holes around the center frame. Remember to work on the self-healing cutting mat and mouse pad. *Chain stitch* the holes, using yellow pearl thread.

5. Center a photo under the frame and secure it with one side of double-sided tacky tape. Leave the paper backing on the other side of the tape for now.

POCKET

1. Copy the pocket pattern (page 111). Transfer the pattern for the foam bottom to yellow craft foam. Transfer the pattern for the paper top to decorative paper. Cut them out using the craft knife and ruler.

2. Spray the back of the paper pocket with adhesive and stick it to the top of the yellow foam pocket. Refer to the pattern for placement.

3. If you haven't transferred the stitch guides yet, transfer them onto the assembled pocket. Use the paper piercer to poke holes about 1/8" (3 mm) apart along the dashed line.

4. *Backstitch* the lines, using orange pearl thread. Sew the pink button to the top of the pocket, using yellow pearl thread.

ATTACH THE FRAME AND POCKET

1. Test the arrangement on your scrapbook page. Remove the paper backing from the tape on the back of the frame, and secure it in place.

2. Place three strips of double-sided tacky tape along the bottom and lower sides of the pocket back. Align the pocket over the frame on your page and firmly stick it down.

3. Hold down the outside edges of the pocket and, with the paper piercer, re-poke holes along the 1" (2.5 cm) upper sides of the frame, so that you will be able to stitch through the back of the scrapbook page.

4. *Backstitch* the upper sides, going through the same holes as the first stitches, using orange pearl thread. Secure the thread at the back of the scrapbook page with a piece of tape.

You'll need

- ✓ Decorative paper
- ✓ Yellow cardstock
- ✓ Yellow craft foam
- ✓ Blue craft foam
- ✓ Tangerine mesh
- ✓ Craft knife
- ✓ Ruler
- ✓ Chenille needle, size 22
- ✓ Cotton pearl thread, size 5: orange and yellow
- ✓ Paper piercer
- ✓ Mouse pad
- ✓ Self-healing cutting mat
- ✓ Double-sided tacky tape
- ✓ Spray adhesive
- ✓ Pink button

It's Easy — When You Know How

Get Ready

Embroidery doesn't require a lot of expensive materials or machines. Basically, you need something to stitch on, threads, needles, and some notions. The right tools and materials can make projects go a lot easier and faster and will help you achieve better results, too. Let's go shopping!

FABRICS

There's a world of fabric out there for you to embroider. Pull something from your closet, a thrift store (great old linens), or the sale rack. (You can stitch on paper, too; more on that later.) Some fabrics are easier to stitch on than others, but with a few pointers and a little practice, you can get great results on almost any fabric.

For your very first project, pick a solid-color fabric with a stable, even weave, such as an all-cotton bandanna, linen napkin, or tea towel. A plain fabric will help you see the way the stitches are being formed. Also, start with a flat object or piece of fabric, not something like jeans. When you're happy with the way your stitches are turning out, try embroidering on printed fabric.

Embellished T-shirts are so hot, you have to do one. Luckily, standard cotton T-shirts are a good choice for embroidery because they have a smooth knit with no ridges. Knit fabric is trickier to embroider than woven fabric because it stretches. We don't recommend stitching over stretchy fabrics or fabrics with large ridges.

Tip

You can embellish just about anything with embroidery, even things you just can't stitch through. Just make an appliqué first (page 22) and then glue it on.

Sheets, pillowcases, and other linens are begging for embroidery. However, you need to use a fine needle and embroidery floss, rather than pearl thread, for linens with high thread counts.

Denim is a natural choice for updated embroidery designs. Although it is tough to work the needle in and out of this dense fabric, with the right needle, a needle puller, and a few tips, you can do it. When working on denim:

- Pick an area on the garment where you will stitch through one layer of fabric. If you want to embellish a yoke, cuff, or collar, you will be stitching through two or more layers and doing some serious tugging on the needle. (In fact, stitching through more than one layer is usually more difficult whatever the fabric.)
- Use the smallest needle you can thread two strands of embroidery floss into, and choose embroidery floss rather than pearl cotton.
- Since denim can be extra tough, sometimes it's easier to support the fabric with your fingers rather than using an embroidery hoop. Try it and see which works better for you.

Tip

Be sure to follow specific laundering instructions for the fiber you're using. For example, silk has to be dry-cleaned.

Before you start, wash whatever you're going to stitch on to remove sizing and prevent shrinking and puckering later. Follow the guidelines for laundering on the manufacturer's care label.

Press the fabric or item with a clean iron, from the wrong side whenever possible. Ironing fabric before cutting will help you cut it more accurately. Pressing and starching the fabric before stitching will give you a smoother, more stable surface, making stitching easier and better looking.

THREADS

Every color imaginable! Sheen and sparkle! Choosing and working with threads is pure enjoyment.

You'll want to buy good thread. DMC and Anchor are high-quality, reliable brands that produce great results. These brands are colorfast, which means they will not bleed onto the fabric when they are wet. Quality brands of thread won't shrink and cause your project to pucker. Floss and thread are inexpensive. Avoid "bargain" brands that can give you much more trouble than you bargained for.

• • •

Pearl thread (1). The quintessential thread for beginners. Everybody loves cotton pearl thread's lustrous sheen and vast color selection. It's thicker than embroidery floss and is tightly twisted so you use it as one thread. You can't and shouldn't try to separate strands.

Six-strand embroidery floss (2). Floss is available in lots of fibers: 100 percent cotton, linen, silk, and rayon, to name a few. It comes in almost every color you can imagine, even unusual hand-dyed colors. When you separate floss into individual strands and recombine them, you can achieve a variety of effects depending on the number of strands used. One strand produces very fine lines and delicate details. All six strands can be used to create thick, bold stitches.

Metallic thread, specialty threads, and other fun fibers (3). These are the icing on the cake! When you feel confident about your skill with cotton pearl thread and floss, practice with silk (yum!) thread for a while before you try to work with metallic or other specialty threads. Silk is slippery, but it's a lot easier to handle than many other specialty threads. Metallic and specialty threads tend to fray, untwist, tangle, or snag after a while. The first line of defense is to use short lengths of thread. Use a slightly larger needle than you would normally, so it makes a hole big enough not to "rough up" the thread. As soon as you notice that the thread is looking thinner, frayed, or worn, end that thread and begin again with a fresh thread. Despite their trickiness, don't hesitate to embroider with these sweet threads. The more you stitch with them, the more you'll love using them. Use a thread conditioner to keep things moving along smoothly.

• • •

Before you know it, you'll have lots of threads and flosses. What's the best way to keep everything organized so you can find what you want for your next project? We keep each color of floss or thread in an individual, snack size, resealable plastic bag. Write the color number on the outside of the bag with a fine-tip permanent marker. We like to save the label with the color number and brand information in the bag as well. The plastic bags keep your threads clean, dry, and fuzz free and will keep small humans and pet friends safe. (We learned about this danger the hard way after paying $1,000 to have embroidery floss surgically removed from our cat Toby's stomach!)

When you've amassed a collection of little plastic bags of thread, organize them by color into a small storage box. Plastic shoe boxes with snap-on lids or photo storage boxes work well for this. Label each box with the colors that it contains. Storage units with shallow drawers are handy for storing thread, too.

NEEDLES

The right needle will make embroidering delightful; the wrong needle makes it harder than it has to be. A needle's job is to make a hole in the fabric that the thread can pass through easily, so the thread doesn't drag and wear down. If the needle is too narrow, the thread will fray and break. If the needle is too wide, you can have trouble getting it through your fabric, it might leave holes, and your stitches will look sloppy.

Needles don't cost a lot, so buy the best quality you can find. Cheap needles can have burrs on them and they often bend, snap, and rust easily. It's time to throw out a needle when it feels rough or won't pull through your fabric smoothly.

The right size of needle depends on the size of the thread. The correct size needle should be slightly wider at the eye (the hole for the thread) than the thickness of your thread. For help selecting the size of needle, see the project instructions or the chart on page 72.

Store needles in a pincushion, wool/felt needle book, or wooden tube needle case to keep them sharp, clean, dry, and free from corrosion.

• • •

Crewel or embroidery needles (1). These have a sharp point for piercing fabric. They have an elongated oval eye that makes it easy to thread stranded embroidery floss. Some companies use the name "crewel" on their packaging for embroidery needles.

Chenille needles (2). These also have a sharp point that will pierce through fabric and other threads, but they are thicker and longer and have a longer, bigger eye than crewel needles. The large eye allows you to thread pearl cotton, yarn, thick threads, or stranded embroidery floss.

Tapestry needles (3). Similar to chenille needles, these needles have a blunt tip. They are used for stitches worked in the surface threads, such as the whipping on running and backstitches or the weaving on woven and double-woven backstitches. Tapestry needles are also used for most paper crafts.

Beading needles (4). Longer and thinner than ordinary sewing needles, beading needles are about the same diameter the whole length, with a tiny round eye that beads can easily pass over.

Sharps (5). These are general sewing needles. They have small round eyes and sharp points.

Crewel or Embroidery Needle Sizes	Floss Strands
10	one strand of six-stranded floss
8	three strands of six-stranded floss
3	six strands of six-stranded floss
6	#5 pearl cotton

Tapestry and Chenille Needle Sizes	Floss Strands
26	one or two strands of six-stranded floss
24	three or four strands of six-stranded floss
22	six strands of six-stranded floss
22	#5 pearl cotton

1   2   3   4   5

CUTTING TOOLS

You'll need some simple cutting tools. Shears have a small handle for your thumb and a larger handle for your other fingers. Scissors have same-sized handles. If you're stitching on paper, you'll need a few special tools; see the section on paper (page 96).

. . .

Craft scissors and shears (1). Have a pair of these on hand, too. They're for cutting paper, cardstock, and other things that you shouldn't cut with your embroidery scissors or fabric shears.

Embroidery scissors (2). With small blades and very sharp, tiny, pointed tips, embroidery scissors are used for trimming threads and snipping out bad stitches. Never use them for anything else. Keep them in a sheath or case to protect them and yourself.

Fabric shears (3). These should only be used for cutting fabric and threads; they will become dull if they are used to cut paper.

Tip

You might want to label your shears "FABRIC ONLY" with a permanent marker so nobody ruins them by mistake.

NOTIONS

These little notions can make a big difference. They can make your stitches look great, and make embroidering easier, too.

• • •

Sponge (1). Some stitchers like to use a small sponge to moisten threads before threading into a needle and to straighten threads. The sponge must be perfectly clean and should be dedicated to this use only.

Tip

The world can be a messy place. Wash your hands before you start to work on a project; then keep food and drinks far away from your embroidery. Carry a few individually packaged hand wipes in your project kit and you'll be ready to make a clean start when you're on the go. When you're not working on your project, store it in a resealable plastic bag to keep it clean and dry.

Tip

Keep your supplies in a portable storage container so you'll have everything ready whenever and wherever you've got the itch to stitch!

Needle threadesr (2). Have trouble threading a needle? Try this fine wire loop that passes through the eye of the needle easily. You just insert the thread into the wire loop and slowly pull the needle threader back through the eye of the needle.

Needle puller (3). A small rubber disc helps you "get a grip" on your needle when you're having trouble pulling the needle through the fabric.

Thimbles and needle pushers (4). These protect the middle finger of your stitching hand—or the finger you use to push the needle—while you're embroidering. Our favorite thimble is a leather quilting thimble with a small metal disk at the fingertip. It's open at the top for your nail tip to stick out. A steel thimble is needed to embroider on denim or other tough fabric. The indentations on the surface of a steel thimble hold the needle in place while you push it through the fabric. You might start out without a thimble, but when your finger gets sore, you'll be happy you've got one on hand (so to speak).

Thread conditioner (5). This product helps prevent fraying and tangling. It's especially helpful when using metallic and specialty threads. You simply draw the thread across the conditioner and then smooth it with your fingers. Our favorite conditioner is Thread Heaven.

TOOLS AND TIPS FOR PATTERN TRANSFER

All the patterns for the projects are at the back of the book. You can use a scanner and printer or a photocopy machine to make a copy of the pattern. That way you'll save the original pattern to use again for another project. A computer or copy machine will also allow you to resize the pattern for your project. If the pattern is for a template or stencil, print it onto cardstock and cut it out with craft scissors. Cut any inner shapes using a craft knife and self-healing cutting mat.

There are lots of options for transferring the pattern to fabric. The project you're doing will determine which method you should use. Always read and follow the manufacturer's instructions for applying and removing the marks. If you wing it, you can run into problems. The numbers below refer to the photo.

. . .

Transfer mesh (1). Trace the pattern onto the mesh with pencil. Then place the mesh over the right side of the fabric, and draw over the lines with the desired fabric marker. The marker will go through the holes in the mesh and onto the fabric.

Heat transfer pens and pencils (2). Trace the mirror image of the pattern onto paper. Then place the image facedown on the right side of the fabric, and press it with an iron to transfer the marks to the fabric.

White chalk pencil (3). Use with the transfer mesh, stencil, or template on dark-colored fabrics. Marks not covered with embroidery can be brushed or washed away.

Water-erasable marker (4). Use with transfer mesh, stencil, or template. Marks can be washed away with a few drops of water.

Air-erasable marker (5). Use with transfer mesh, stencil, or template. Marks will disappear after about 48 hours, so use this method when you will be able to complete your project in this time.

Wax-free dressmaker's tracing paper (6). This comes in sheets; colors are shown in the small samples. Tape the tracing paper facedown on the right side of the fabric; tape the pattern faceup over the tracing paper. Trace the pattern with a ballpoint pen so you can see whether you have traced all the lines. Marks not covered by embroidery can be brushed away or erased.

Light box (not shown). You can place a sheer fabric over the pattern on a light box or bright window and trace directly onto the fabric, using a marking pencil or pen.

HOOPS

Fabric mounted in an embroidery hoop is easier to work with. A hoop holds your fabric tight from all directions while you're stitching. It helps you keep the size of your stitches even and keeps you from pulling your stitches too tight, which makes the fabric pucker.

Embroidery hoops come in an assortment of styles and sizes. Wood and plastic hoops have an adjustable screw on the outer ring; metal ones just have a spring. Whenever you can, select a hoop large enough to fit the whole design so the fabric won't have to be moved during stitching. The pressure of the rings can crush stitches when the hoop has to be moved around to the other areas of the design.

To help keep fabric taut and to protect delicate fabric, wrap cotton twill tape around the inner ring. Secure the end with a few stitches. If your fabric is very delicate, or you need to place the hoop on stitches, wrap the top hoop, too.

Tip

Take your project out of the hoop when you aren't working on it to prevent permanent dents or distortions in your fabric.

Here's how to put the fabric in a hoop:

1. Lay the smaller, inner ring on a flat surface. Center your design, right side up, over the inner ring.
2. Lay the outer adjustable ring over the fabric. It's a good idea to position the screw at the top of your project so your thread doesn't get caught on it as you stitch. Lefties locate the screw on the right side of the top, righties on the left side of the top. Press the outer ring down with even pressure until it is secure.
3. Tighten the screw until the outer ring fits snugly over the inner ring and fabric.

Working around the hoop, gently pull the fabric evenly from all sides until it is taut but not too tight. The fabric should feel and sound like a drumhead when you flick it with your fingertip.

Get Set

PREPARE THE FLOSS OR THREAD

When you open a new skein:

1. Remove the labels and save the label that has the color number on it.
2. Untwist the pearl thread. Lay out the pearl thread or floss into an oval shape.
3. Cut through the pearl thread strands at both ends of the oval, so you have two bundles of 12" (30.5 cm) pieces. Cut through the floss at one end of the oval, so you have one bundle of 12" (30.5 cm) pieces.

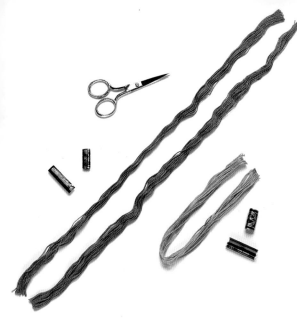

Often you need to separate one, two, or more strands of floss from a six-strand length. To keep them from tangling, remove just one strand of floss at a time. After cutting the floss into 12" (30.5 cm) pieces (above), hold the top of one piece in your hand. Use the other hand to separate one end from the group. Pull that strand straight up and out from the rest. The remaining strands will probably bunch up as you remove it, but you can easily smooth them back in place. Repeat the process to remove each individual strand that you need.

Floss should be straightened before stitching to produce smooth, even stitches. Straightening is also an effective way to revive threads that are creased from being tightly wound on a cardboard or plastic bobbin or for threads that have been crumpled up. Slightly moisten each individual strand with a drop of water; use the tips of your fingers (or a small, damp sponge) to smooth out and spread the moisture along the length of the strand. The strand should be barely moist, not wet, and should dry completely before you thread your needle.

You can blend strands to create customized colors and special effects like the shimmering wings on the spa mask (page 36). First, straighten each individual strand. Then lay out the straightened strands with the ends aligned, and smooth them out along their length. Don't twist the strands. Skim the group as one combined strand across the surface of a thread conditioner. Thread your needle and trim both ends even. Beginners might find it easier to start stitching by tying a small tight knot at the end of the combined strand to help hold all of the strands together.

THREAD THE NEEDLE

Through the ages, millions of needles have been threaded by people who put the end of the thread into their mouths to wet the tip. Many discerning needleworkers use a small sponge and water for moistening thread. Either way will work. Once the tip of the thread is moistened, use your embroidery scissors to snip the tip, either at an angle or straight across. Pinch the tip, aim, and thread it through the needle eye.

Having a little trouble? Try threading the needle from its other side. Occasionally, a needle eye is smaller on one side than the other. Still no luck? Don't get frustrated. Try using a time-saving and very inexpensive needle threader (page 74).

TIPS FOR GOOD STITCHES

Now you're ready to start stitching! Use a straight up-and-down stabbing motion, pulling the thread all the way through to the front or back with each motion. It will help you to keep your stitches and tension (how tight you pull the thread) even.

Aim for equal-sized stitches and consistent tension. Your stitches should be flat against the fabric, neither loopy and loose nor tight and scrunching up the fabric. Here are some tips:

- Put the "how to" illustration of the stitch you're learning where you can see it, and refer to it as you take each step.
- Before starting a project, try the stitches that are new to you on a scrap of fabric until you're happy about the way they look. Almost everyone needs a little practice.
- Start all of your stitches on the wrong side of the fabric.
- Use a hoop whenever you can.
- The normal motions of stitching often cause the thread to tangle. When your thread becomes twisted, let the needle hang down and dangle freely until the thread unwinds itself. It's a good idea to do this every once in a while even if you don't think you need to.

Tip

Nobody's perfect! To recover from a bad stitch or two, simply remove the needle from your thread. Then, working from the wrong side of the fabric, use the needle to loosen the thread and undo the stitch. Rethread your needle with the same thread, redo the stitch, and get back to work. To correct more than a few bad stitches, use your embroidery scissors to clip the stitches on the wrong side of the fabric, taking care not to cut the fabric. Use tweezers to pick out the stitches from the right side. Pull free a 2" (5 cm) tail of thread and thread it back onto the needle on the wrong side. Weave the tail under the back of some of the remaining good stitches.

KNOTS AND TAILS

For projects where the underside of the embroidery will never be seen, it's okay to tie a small knot in the end of the thread to anchor the first stitch. Do this by wrapping the thread end once around the tip of your index finger. Then, using your thumb, roll the thread off your finger, twisting it into a small knot. When the thread gets too short or you finish a stitching line, pull the needle to the underside and take a couple tiny stitches where they won't show before cutting the thread.

There are some projects, however—like napkins or a handkerchief—where people will see both sides of your embroidery. Here are ways to start without knots and hide the tails so the wrong side looks almost as good as the right side.

For a knot-free beginning, use a "waste knot."

1. Make a knot at the end of your thread.
2. Insert the needle on the *right side* of the fabric about 2" (5 cm) from your starting point on the pattern line where your stitching will be heading.
3. Bring the needle up from the wrong side of the fabric at your starting point. The knot will be on the right side and the thread will trail under the pattern line on the wrong side.
4. Work your stitches, crossing over the thread on the wrong side to secure it.
5. Just before you reach the knot, snip it off. That's where the name "waste" knot comes from.

If you already have some stitching done, simply weave your needle under the back (wrong side) of a few stitches of the same or similar color before bringing the needle to the right side at the start of a line. To hide the tail at the end of a line, weave the needle under several stitches of the same or similar color and snip off the remaining bit of the tail close to the fabric. When the stitches are too large or loose to hold the thread securely, make a few backstitches through the threads on the wrong side of the fabric.

FINISHING TOUCH

When you finish stitching, remove any pattern transfer marks from your fabric, following the directions that came with the transfer product (page 75). And last but not least, here is the seasoned stitcher's secret finishing touch that makes your embroidery pop: Press the embroidery from the back side.

1. Lay a white terry cloth towel on the ironing board, and place the embroidery facedown on the towel.
2. Spray over the stitching lightly with spray starch.
3. Press from the center of the embroidery moving out toward the edges.
4. Flip the fabric over and admire your spectacular embellishment!

Tip

You accidentally prick your finger and get a drop of blood on your fabric; what do you do? Don't let it dry. Immediately cut a length of light-colored thread, roll it into a ball, and put it in your mouth, wetting it with your own saliva. Lay a paper towel or white terry cloth towel under the embroidery to act as a blotter. Then rub the wet ball of thread over the blood spot. The enzymes in your saliva react with your own blood to dissolve it. Follow by rinsing the spot with cold water. Press a clean white towel on the wet spot to help it dry quickly.

Stitch

Here are instructions for all the stitches used in these projects. Don't worry that you have to learn them all right away. In fact, you can make lots of fabulous designs with only one simple stitch. When you're ready for more, though, there are many easy stitches that create special effects for your projects.

STRAIGHT STITCH

creates a little dash

Bring the needle up to the right side of the fabric at your starting point. Insert the needle the desired distance from the starting point; then pull it to the back of the fabric. That's it.

Cross-stitch is simply one diagonal straight stitch across another, with the stitches crossing in the center. For long lines of cross-stitches, work all the diagonal stitches in one direction and then turn around and work the stitches in the other direction. The cross-stitches in this book are free-form, unlike counted cross-stitches that require a chart or special even-weave fabric.

RUNNING STITCH

creates a broken dash-space-dash line

Bring the needle up to the right side of the fabric at your starting point. Push the needle in and out of the fabric along the pattern line, leaving a space between each stitch. Keep the stitches an even size and tension for a consistent look.

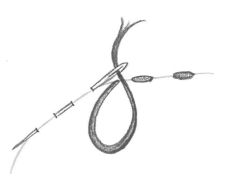

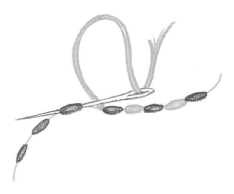

Top to bottom:
running stitch,
double running stitch,
alternating double
running stitch

DOUBLE RUNNING STITCH

creates a solid line of end-to-end dashes; you can use a
different color for each line of stitches to make a solid line
of alternating colored dashes

Stitch a line of evenly spaced running stitches. Using the same holes, stitch another row of running stitches, filling in the empty spaces left by the first line of stitches.

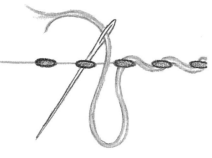

WHIPPED RUNNING STITCH

creates a solid, raised, narrow, twisted line

Stitch a base row of running stitches. Thread a tapestry needle with the "whipping" thread, and bring the needle up to the right side at the starting point of the base row of running stitches. Lace the tapestry needle under a running stitch, whip the thread over it, then lace the thread under the next running stitch. Repeat.

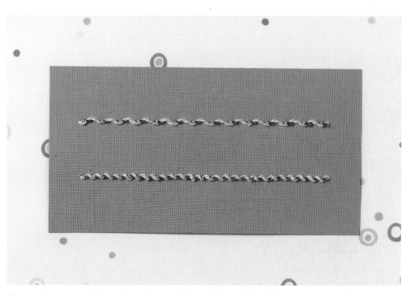

Top to bottom: whipped running stitch, whipped double running stitch

WHIPPED DOUBLE RUNNING STITCH

creates a solid, raised, twisted line that looks like a small cord

Make a base line of double running stitches. Begin the whipping step at the starting point of the base row. Use a tapestry needle to lace under a stitch, whip the thread over it, then lace the thread under the following running stitch.

SATIN STITCH

very closely placed, side-by-side, straight stitches; used to fill shapes

Bring the thread up to the right side of your fabric precisely on the pattern line. Insert the needle straight across the shape, on the opposite side. Bring the needle out again as close as possible to the end of the first stitch. Insert the needle into the fabric straight across the shape in the opposite direction to form the next satin stitch. Repeat to fill the shape.

To pad satin stitches: Stitch split stitches (page 92) around the outline of the shape; then fill in the shape with small running stitches (page 83) to create a base. Use either straight or diagonal satin stitches from pattern line to pattern line over the outline to create a raised, padded look.

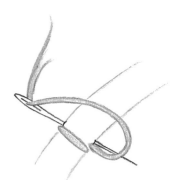

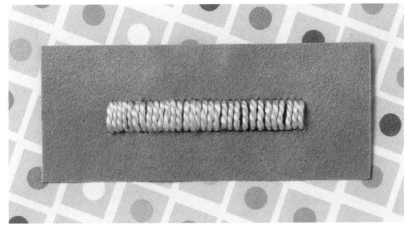

Satin stitch

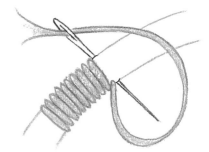

COUCHING

tiny stitches from one thread hold another thread in place

The thread that is sewn down is called the laid thread. The couching thread is the thread that sews the laid thread into place. Use a large chenille needle to bring the laid thread (whatever you're wanting to couch down) up to the front of the fabric at your starting point. Secure the laid thread onto the pattern line with pins or a tiny bit of fabric glue. Where you want to end the couching, "plunge" the laid thread through to the wrong side of the fabric. Secure the ends of the laid thread on the wrong side of the fabric with a few stitches from the couching thread. Bring the needle threaded with the couching thread up very close to the laid thread. Insert the needle down on the opposite side of the laid thread to make a stitch perpendicular to it. Bring the needle up into position for another perpendicular stitch. Take evenly spaced stitches over the laid thread until you reach its end. When you're finished stitching, dab a tiny drop of fabric glue onto the tails of the couching thread.

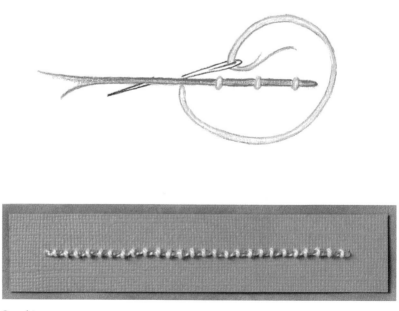

Couching

CORAL STITCH

creates a solid dash-knot-dash line

Bring the needle up to the right side of the fabric at your starting point. Make a tiny perpendicular stitch (through just a few threads of the fabric) across your pattern line. Keep the needle in the fabric; don't pull the thread through yet. Loop the thread over and under the needle tip. Then pull the thread through the loop, forming a knot.

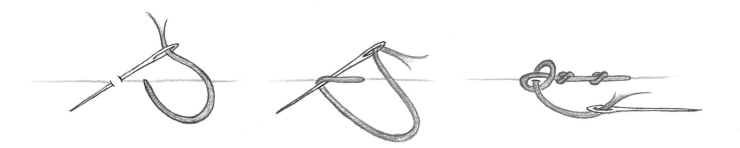

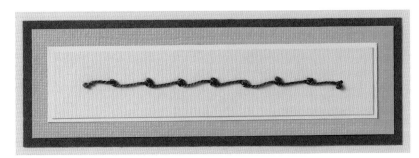

Coral stitch

CHAIN STITCH

looks like a chain

Bring the needle up to the right side of the fabric at your starting point. Hold the thread toward you with your free thumb, take a stitch into the same hole where the thread was brought up, forming a small loop. Bring the needle up through the fabric where you want the end of the stitch but do not pull the thread through yet. Bring the needle out and over the loop. Use your free hand to guide the thread around the needle making a second loop overlapping the first one. Repeat.

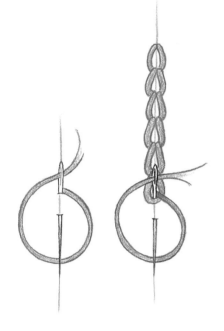

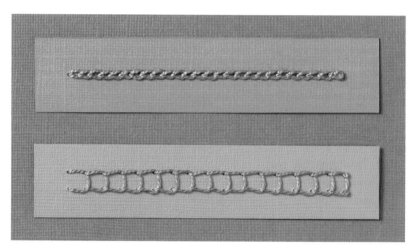

Top to bottom: chain stitch, square chain stitch

SQUARE CHAIN STITCH

creates a wide "ladder" looking stitch that can be laced with ribbon or other fibers

Draw two parallel lines where you want to stitch. You can use a line of stitching that is already on a garment as one of the guidelines, or stitch across a seam that has two parallel lines of stitching. You'll be stitching downward between the two parallel guidelines.

Bring the needle up to the right side of the fabric at your starting point on the left line. Insert the needle on the right line, directly across from your starting point; then in the same motion, bring the needle out under the starting point on the left line. *Don't pull the needle through yet. Loop the thread under the needle tip, then pull the thread through, but don't pull the thread tight. Leave a loop that you can insert the needle into to form the next stitch. Insert the needle into the right line, directly across from the emerging thread. Bring your needle up on the left line underneath the emerging thread. Repeat from * to the end of the line.

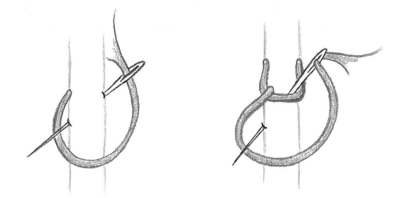 

BLANKET STITCH

is often used as an embellishment and to secure the edges of appliqués

Insert the needle from the right side of the fabric through to the back. Bring the needle up while holding the loop of thread with your left thumb. Make a vertical stitch, bringing the needle out over the loop made by the thread. Pull the needle through until the blanket stitch is snug against the fabric.

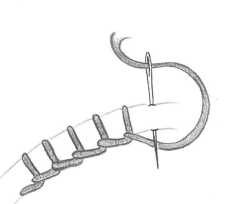

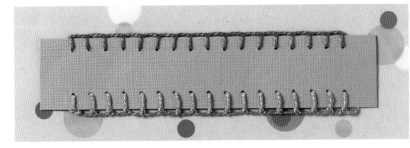

Top to bottom: blanket stitch, knotted blanket stitch

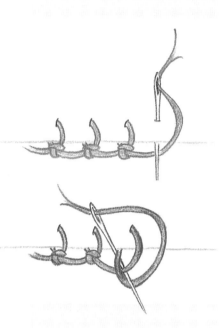

KNOTTED BLANKET STITCH

just like blanket stitch with a tiny knot at each stitch

Working from left to right on the edge of the fabric, bring the needle up from the back a bit from the edge and make a blanket stitch. Before moving to the next blanket stitch, loop the needle behind the two threads that hang from the edge of the fabric. To keep even tension, you may find it helpful to hold the top of the blanket stitch while you make the knot. Repeat as you would for the blanket stitch, inserting the needle into the right side of the fabric and taking the next stitch a bit to the right of the previous stitch.

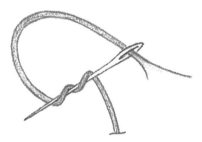

FRENCH KNOTS

create a raised, round dot that looks like a bead

Bring the needle up through to the right side of the fabric. With your free hand, grip the thread about 2" (5 cm) from the spot and pull it taut but not tight. Wind the thread that is between your fingers and the fabric around the needle once. Continue holding the thread taut, while inserting the needle back into the starting point hole (or very close to it). Pull the thread through the wound loop and fabric to the wrong side. Secure the thread after each French knot. For larger knots, wind the thread around the needle two or three times. These are also called bullion stitches.

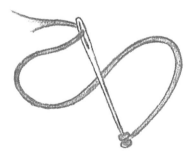

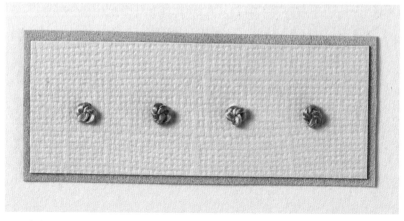

French knots

BACKSTITCH

creates a solid line of end-to-end dashes

Bring the needle up to the right side of the fabric one stitch length from the starting point. Insert the needle at the starting point. Then bring it up again, two stitch lengths away. Pull the thread through, making a stitch. Repeat the first step, inserting your needle at the end of the stitch you just made.

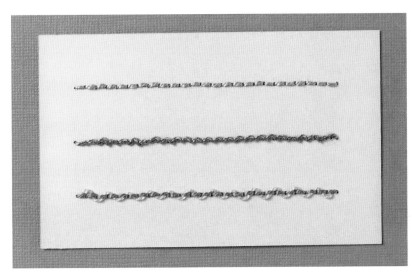

Top to bottom: backstitch, whipped backstitch, woven backstitch

WHIPPED BACKSTITCH

creates a raised, twisted line that looks like a small cord.

Make a base line of backstitches. Begin the whipping step at the starting point of the base row. Use a tapestry needle to lace under a backstitch, whip the thread over it, then lace the thread under the following backstitch.

WOVEN BACKSTITCH

an extra thread snakes back and forth under the backstitches

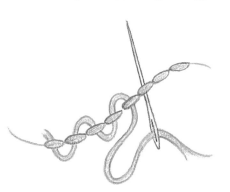

Stitch a base row of backstitches. Use a tapestry needle to weave under a backstitch from the top to the bottom. Then weave under the following stitch from the bottom to the top.

DOUBLE WOVEN BACKSTITCH

two extra threads snake back and forth under the backstitches

Stitch a row of woven backstitches. Start a new thread working the same way as the woven backstitch, filling in the empty spaces on the opposite side.

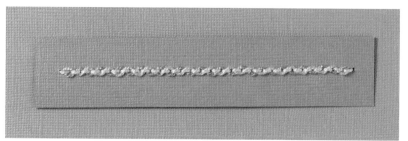

Double woven backstitch

SPLIT STITCH

looks like a small tight chain stitch.

Make a small straight stitch. Then bring the needle to the right side again halfway along the stitch you've just made, splitting the thread with the tip of the needle. Repeat to the end of the line.

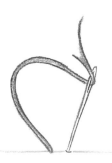

STEM STITCH

looks like a narrow twisted cord

Bring the needle up on your pattern line and take a small stitch. Come back up close alongside the last stitch, at about the halfway point of the stitch. Take another stitch and come up alongside it. Repeat to the end of the line.

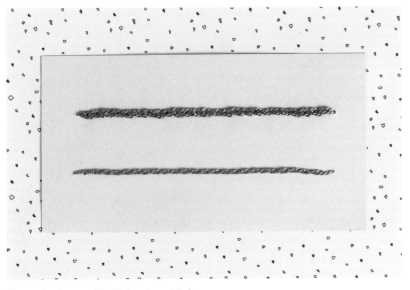

Top to bottom: split stitch, stem stitch

WHIPPED STEM STITCH

looks like a slightly raised cord.

Stem stitch a base line. Begin the whipping step at the starting point of the base line. Use a tapestry needle to lace under a stitch, whip the thread over it, then lace the thread under the following stitch.

Get Creative

ADD BEADS

Beads add a little sparkle and dimension to your embroidery. Simply thread up a beading needle with beading thread and stitch beads into your embroidered design. Here's how:

- A single bead can be added by sliding it onto your beading needle down the thread to the fabric. When you insert your needle back into the fabric, the bead will be secured in place. Make a small tight knot on the wrong side of the fabric.

- To secure several single beads spaced apart, secure the first one with a stitch and a knot, as above. Then keep your needle threaded and "carry the thread" on the underside of the fabric to the next location. Again, add a bead, stitch and knot. Continue to carry the thread between beads. When you come to the end of your thread, tie a tight double knot. After you've finished attaching all of the beads, snip the carried threads close to the knots.

- For extra protection, put a tiny dab of fabric glue on every knot on the back of your fabric when you're finished beading.

- To attach beads in a line, string four or five beads onto your thread and insert the needle into the fabric after the last bead. Backstitch, bringing the needle up between the first and second beads. Then pass the needle back through the remaining beads again. Add a few more beads and repeat until you have all of your beads in a row.

- To attach a long strand of beads, string the beads; then position the strand on your project and couch (page 86) the strand down, bringing the needle over the strand where it will settle between beads. Skip a few beads between couching stitches, and continue to the end of the line.

Tip

Lay a large towel on your workspace to keep beads from scattering.

ADD PAINT

Painted designs on fabric items can be enhanced with embroidery. Paints formulated especially for use on fabric stay pliable after repeated laundering. You can also mix acrylic craft paints with a textile medium to make them suitable for fabric painting. Some fabric paint has to be heat-set with an iron and some manufacturers recommend waiting 24 hours before laundering the item. Follow the manufacturer's instructions. Here are some of the ways you can apply paint to fabric:

- Wield a brush and freely hand paint whatever you like. Be brave!
- Use fabric paint or craft paint/textile medium mixture for stenciling, too.
- Apply paint to fabric using rubber stamps. Spread a thin layer of paint on a paper plate and dip the stamp into it, or apply paint to the stamp with a foam brush. Always test first. Be sure to clean your rubber stamps thoroughly before the paint dries.

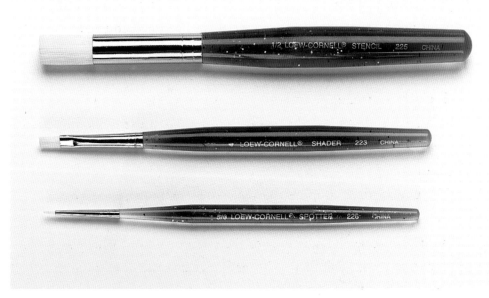

Top to bottom: stencil brush, shader, spotter

STITCH ON PAPER AND CARDSTOCK

Embroidery techniques for fabric can also be used for paper. You can attach vellum and embellishments with stitches. Make a pocket to hold a secret note. Stitch borders and titles and designs. You can stitch letters and words by drawing them freehand or by tracing letter templates or stencils with a disappearing marker. For a finished look, fill the letters in with colored pencil, chalk, or paper paint.

The running stitch and cross-stitch are favorites of paper crafters, but you can do so many more! Play with a variety of embroidery stitches on paper or cardstock before using them on a project. Satin stitch, however, doesn't work well on paper, because the stitches are so close together that the paper tends to tear. The one big trick for stitching on paper and cardstock is to pre-punch the stitching holes. Here's how:

1. Mark the paper/cardstock with dots where you want the stitches to be.
2. Place a self-healing cutting mat on your work surface. On top of that, put your mouse pad, facedown.
3. Put the cardstock on the mouse pad and use a piercer, such as an awl, stiletto, or large chenille needle, to poke holes where you want to stitch.
4. Use a tapestry needle to lace your thread through the holes.
5. Secure the thread on the back of the paper with tape rather than a knot.

Tip

Paper often tears and crumples easily during stitching. Solve that problem by adhering the paper to cardstock with spray adhesive.

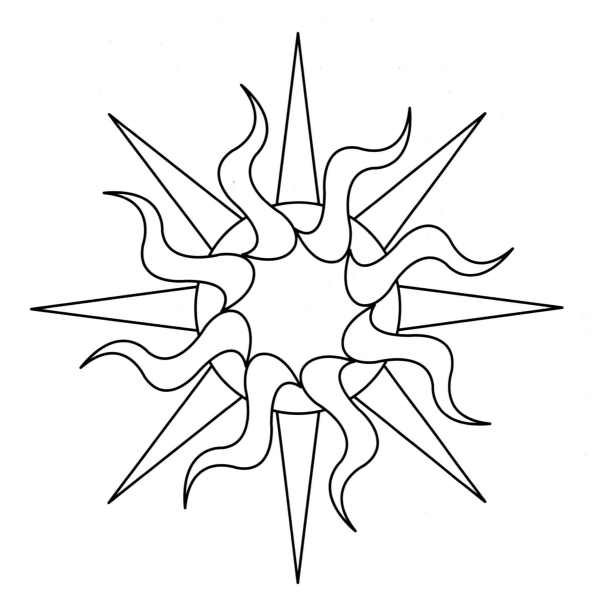

SUN STAR

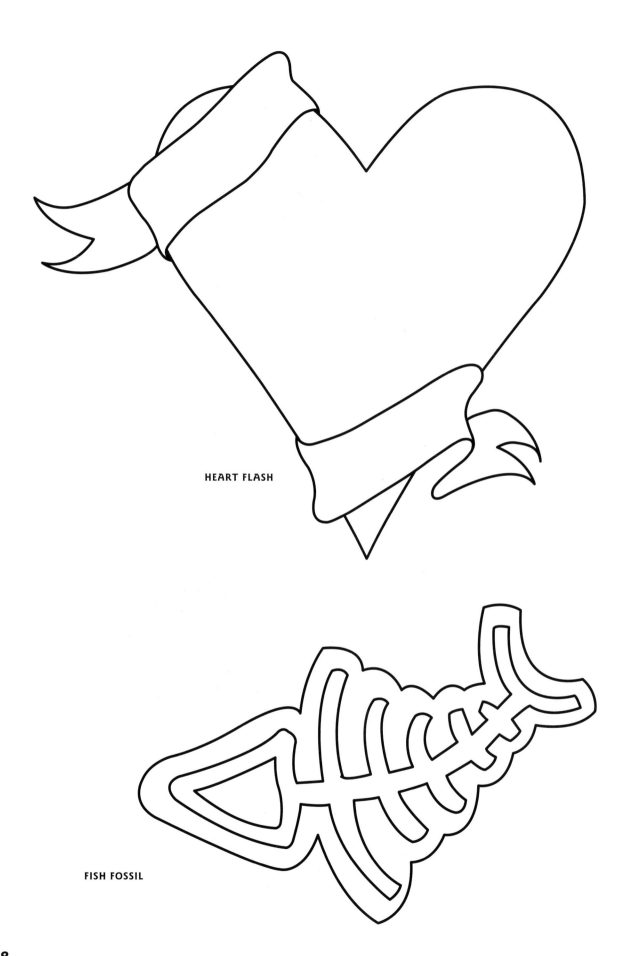

HEART FLASH

FISH FOSSIL

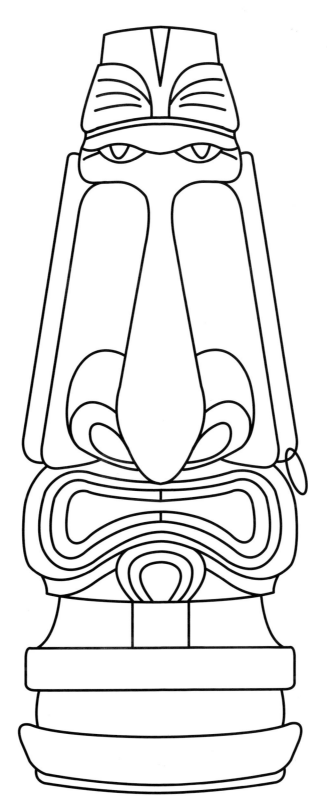

DIRTY MARTINI

ROYAL BEAST

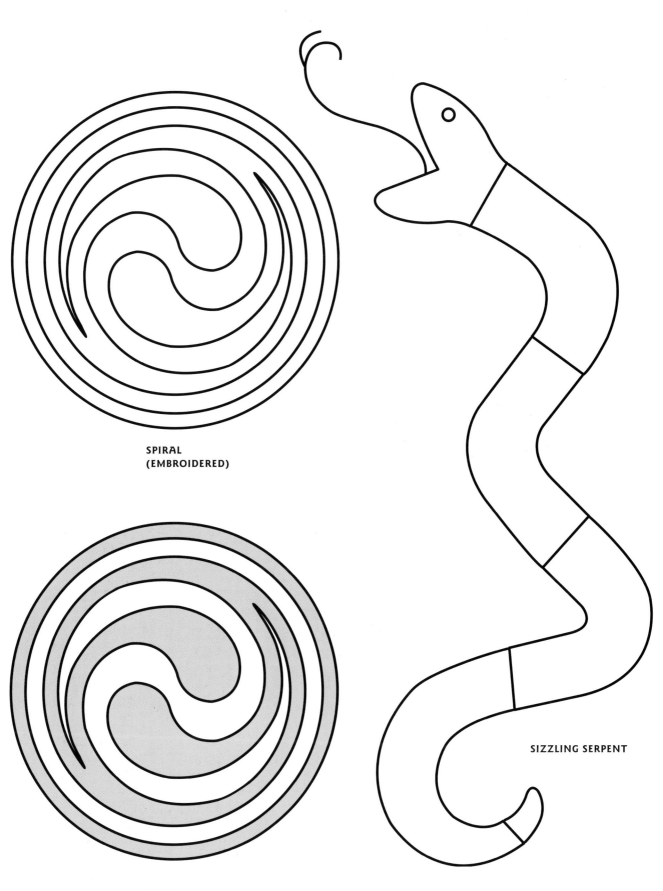

SPIRAL
(EMBROIDERED)

SPIRAL
(APPLIQÚE)

SIZZLING SERPENT

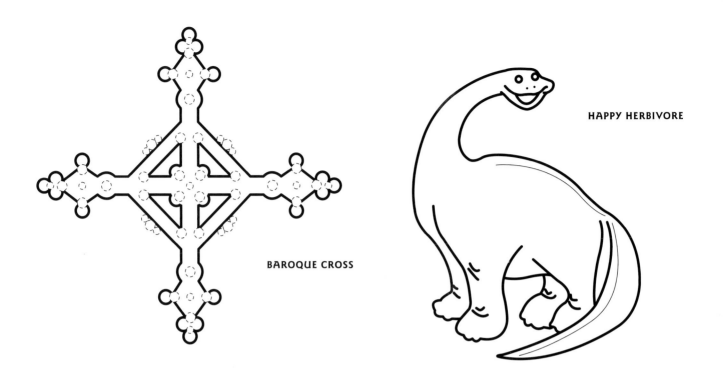

BAROQUE CROSS

HAPPY HERBIVORE

TIME FLIES

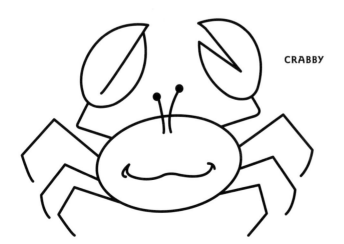

CRABBY

ANKH AMULET

CROWN JEWELS

STEAMY

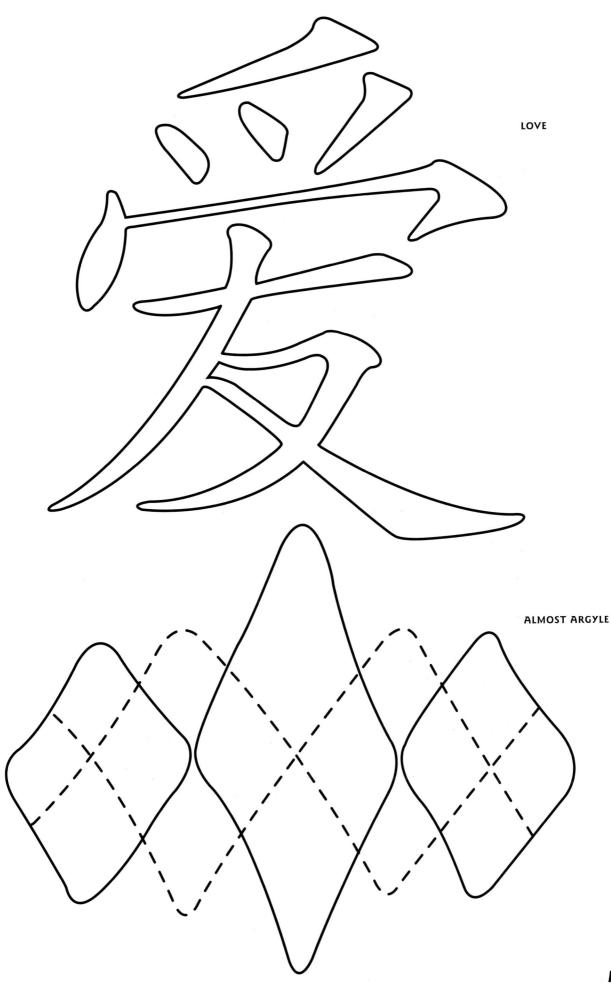

LOVE

ALMOST ARGYLE

105

CELEBRATION

NOTE BOOK

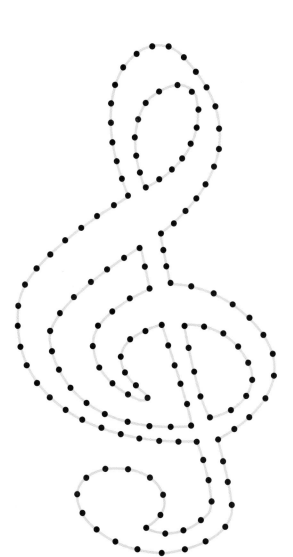

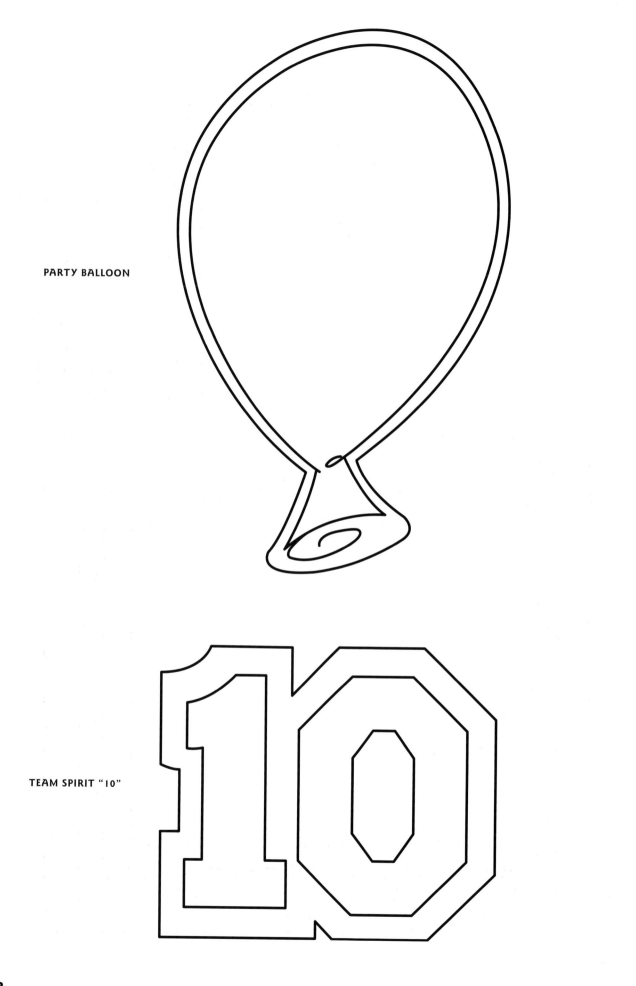

PARTY BALLOON

TEAM SPIRIT "10"

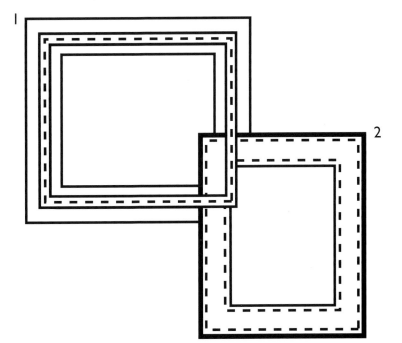

interlocking frame 1

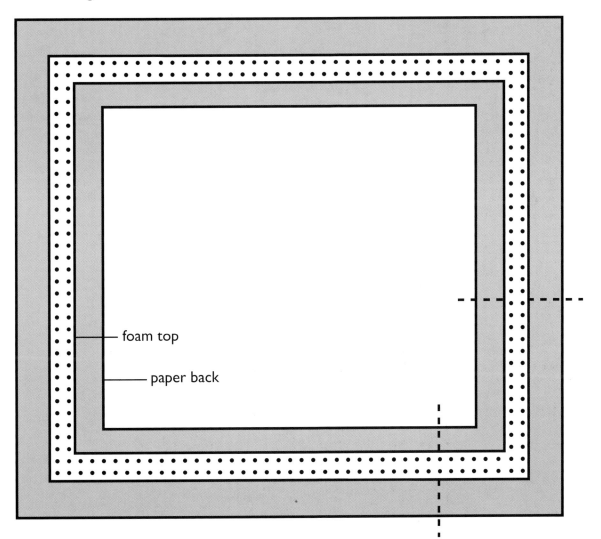

foam top

paper back

SCRAPBOOK FRAMES

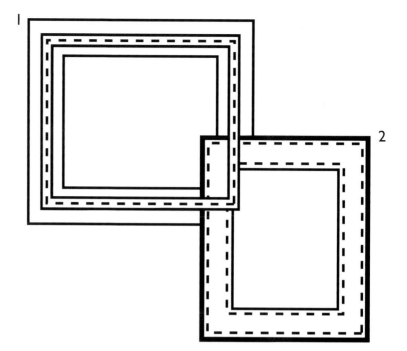

interlocking frame 2

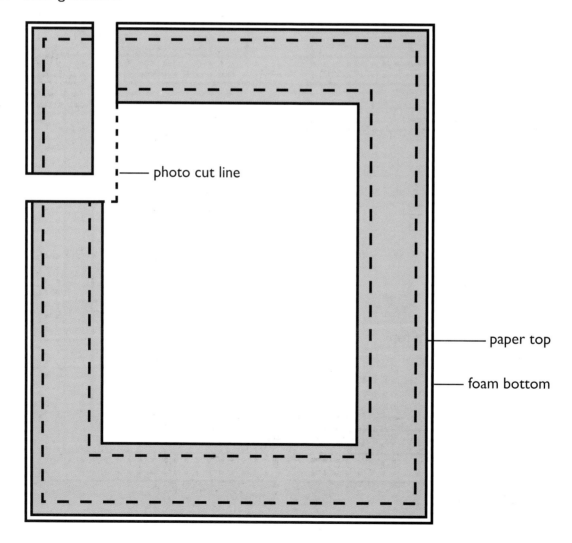

photo cut line

paper top

foam bottom

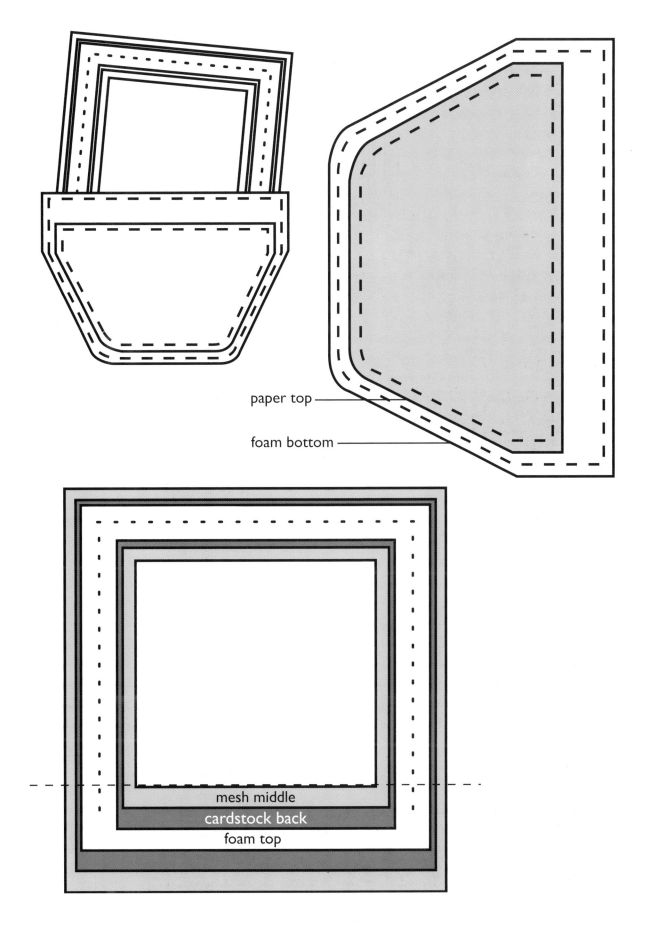

paper top
foam bottom

mesh middle
cardstock back
foam top

Sources

ACKNOWLEDGMENTS

Many thanks to DMC Corporation, Fiskars Brands, Inc., and Loew-Cornell, Inc. for providing materials for this book.

The following products were used for the project:

SUN STAR
DMC Pearl Cotton: yellow 307, dark blue 995, and plum 718

HEART FLASH
DMC Pearl Cotton: red 666 and white blanc

FISH FOSSIL
DMC Pearl Cotton: yellow/green 832 and ivory 677

THE BIG KAHUNA
DMC Pearl Cotton: gold/olive 832, red/orange 606, beige/gray 5644, lemon yellow 445, dark olive green 730, black 310, white blanc, and blue 995

DIRTY MARTINI
DMC Pearl Cotton: dark violet 550, turquoise 959, medium green 907, and dark plum 915
DMC Metallic Floss: silver 5283

ROYAL BEAST
DMC Light Effects Jewels: red E321

SPIRAL (EMBROIDERED)
DMC Pearl Cotton: variegated garnet 115

SPIRAL (APPLIQUÉ)
DMC Light Effects: gold E3821

SIZZLING SERPENT
DMC Pearl Cotton: yellow 307 and green 907
DMC Cotton Embroidery Floss: light orange 970 and black 310

BO HO BEADED BORDER
DMC Pearl Cotton: navy blue 311

BAROQUE CROSS
DMC Light Effects Precious Metals: brown E301
DMC Pearl Cotton: dark brown 3371

ANKH AMULET
DMC Pearl Cotton: gold metallic 5282
DMC Light Effects: gold metallic E3821

DRESS LIKE AN EGYPTIAN
DMC Pearl Cotton: turquoise 597 and medium coral 350
DMC Light Effects: gold metallic E3821
Mill Hill glass seed beads 00557
The Jewelry Shoppe elastic cord BC-07
DMC Metallic Pearl: gold 5282
Wrights Simplicity Trims
Darice, Jewelry Designer bugle beads No. 1102-57

BUTTERFLIES
DMC Pearl Cotton: light nile green 955, medium electric blue 996, very light sky blue 747, very light cranberry 605, light violet 554, and variegated yellow 104
DMC Light Effects: snow white E5200
Mill Hill seed beads

TIME FLIES
DMC Pearl Cotton: yellow 307
Czech Glass Beads from Crafts, Etc!
DMC Cotton Embroidery Floss: medium blue 996, medium lavender 210, and very light blue 747
DMC Light Effects: very light blue E747
Mill Hill seed beads

CROWN JEWELS
DMC Pearl Cotton: lemon yellow 307, light cranberry 604, and medium blue 996

STEAMY
DMC Pearl Cotton: very dark violet 550
DMC Embroidery Floss: very dark violet 550
DMC Light Effects Precious Metals: gold metallic E3821 and pearlescent E5200

CRABBY
DMC Cotton Embroidery Floss: light cranberry 605, lavender 210, yellow-green 772, and black 310

HAPPY HERBIVORE
DMC Light Effects: fluorescent green E990

TEAM SPIRIT "10"
DMC Pearl Cotton: dark navy blue 939, dark red 815, and beige-gray 644

ALMOST ARGYLE
Canvas tote 11" w × 9" h × 3" d (28 × 23 × 7.5 cm)
DMC Pearl Cotton: light tan 739, orange 947, and royal blue 820

LOVE
DMC Pearl Cotton: variegated blue 121

SWEET CONFECTION
DMC Pearl Cotton: pink 604
DMC Light Effects: medium green E966 and white E5200

WEDDING KEEPSAKE
DMC Light Effects: white E5200
Mill Hills seed beads and crystal heart
Swarouski crystal beads, blue crystal bead, and ivory star

EIFFEL TOWER
DMC Linen Floss: pink L778, ligh gold L677, light blue L159, and tan L437

NOTE BOOK
DMC Pearl Cotton: dark yellow 972 and dark lavender 208

CELEBRATION
Periwinkle Whimsy Stripes, Periwinkle Solid Cardstock, Wisteria Dizzy Dots, Wisteria Dots, and Kiwi Solid from Lasting Impressions for Paper, Inc.
DMC Pearl Cotton: pink 604, yellow 444, and lavender 209
DMC Light Effects: pearlescent E5200
Mill Hill seed beads

PARTY BALLOON
DMC Pearl Cotton: aquamarine 943

SCRAPBOOK FRAMES
AP21551 When the Cat's Away; Green, from imagination PROJECT; Amanda's World and Heart Paper, from Daisy D's Paper Co.
DMC Pearl Cotton: dusty rose 962 and white blanc

SCRAPBOOK POCKET
AP21553 Cat's Delight from imagination PROJECT, Amanda's World
DMC Pearl Cotton: orange 922 and yellow 727
Magenta mesh 1003